Slices of Life

A series of stories by student writers in Professor Walt Harrington's journalism class at the University of Illinois published in The News-Gazette. Each story is a short peek into the lives of East Central Illinois residents.

Edited by Walt Harrington

Published by The News-Gazette

The News-Gazette®

EDITOR AND PUBLISHER   John Foreman
EXECUTIVE EDITOR   John Beck
MANAGING EDITOR   Dan Corkery
PHOTO EDITOR   Darrell Hoemann
FEATURES EDITOR   Tony Mancuso

Cover design and book layout: Joan Millis, The News-Gazette

ISBN: 978-0-9846063-8-2

Printed in the United States of America

Library of Congress Cataloging-in-Publication Data

Main entry under title:

Slices of Life: A series of stories by student writers in Professor Walt
    Harrington's journalism class at the University of Illinois published in
    The News-Gazette. Each story is a short peek into the lives of East
    Central Illinois residents. Editor, Walt Harrington

The News-Gazette, Inc.
15 Main Street
Champaign, IL 61820
Phone: (217) 351-5252
Fax: (217) 351-5245
www.news-gazette.com

Dedication

To the people who let us write about them.

Contents

Introduction

The Music of Ordinary Life

"Don't write about Man, write about 'a' man."
E.B. White
"Essays of E.B. White"

The music of ordinary life is everywhere around us. It can be hard to hear, through the traditional blare of robberies, car crashes, politics and scandal, through the too-often angry, shallow and silly voices that screech away on social media. Yet, if you take a moment to listen, you will hear the music: Rabbi Isaac Neuman remembering the good even in the Nazi death camps; Charlie High mourning the death and praising the life of his wife; Gino Baileau struggling to establish his unusual sexual identity; Chike Coleman trying to take joy in every moment of a life debilitated by disease; Bishop Morris Paul Lockett preaching to his abjectly poor congregation; Charlie Sweitzer making a beautiful chair with his hands. These stories — and many more — are collected in *Slices of Life*.

The stories appeared originally in *The News-Gazette* and grew from a collaborative effort between the newspaper and the Department of Journalism at the University of Illinois. The idea was to give aspiring student journalists in my Literary Feature Writing class a taste of real-world experience by seeing their stories appear in the paper and to give the paper's readers more stories that might touch their humanity. The project was supported with grants from the Marajen Stevick Foundation and conducted with the encouragement of the paper's publisher, John Foreman, and the help of features editor Tony Mancuso and *The News-Gazette* photo staff. For three semesters, my class convened at *The News-Gazette* building and included journalism students and the newspaper's professionals. The effort resulted in the "Slice of Life" series that ran in the paper over more than a year. A handful of stories collected here preceded that formal rubric but are still in its tradition. Some of the stories came and went with few comments from the public. Yet many evoked scores of Web "Likes" from readers. The story of Rabbi Neuman alone recorded nearly 400 such "Likes."

The field of journalism has a long tradition of humanized feature reporting and writing. In recent decades, the form has become more sophisticated by integrating drama, telling detail, scene-setting, conversational dialogue, drama, intrigue and emerging insight into its factual storytelling. Ideally, such stories are not collections of information but explorations of ideas through individuals — ambition, grief, hate, creativity, companionship, love (of people, music, birds), faith, excellence, growth. After more than 35 years of writing and editing such stories — from jobs at small local newspapers to *The Washington Post* to book writing and editing — my greatest joy is working with the bright-eyed kids in the Illinois journalism program, knowing that they will go out and someday do memorable journalism themselves. The boundless hope, enthusiasm and talent of my students keeps me young — and on my toes.

At their best, feature stories are "tone poems" that evoke in us a richer understanding of the anonymous people with whom we mingle daily, people who at first glance seem different from us — richer or poorer, younger or older, more educated or less, gay or straight, religious or agnostic, black or white. What such stories are meant to do is remind us that beneath all of that we are much the same. So read the stories in *Slices of Life* and feel the sensation of being inside another human being's skin — his hopes and dreams, her fears and ambitions, the yearning to live a meaningful life.

Because these people are us.

Walt Harrington
Department of Journalism
University of Illinois

Photo by John Dixon/The News-Gazette

1

By faith, Isaac …

By Emily Siner

Some things he wants to remember; some things he tries to forget.

Isaac Neuman remembers a pretty woman who prepared the meals for the supervisors at St. Martin's cemetery, an early Nazi camp in Poland. She took a liking to Isaac. "Stomarek," she called him, a reference to the "one hundred marks" he had tried to hide from his captors. When they found the money, he had received a vicious beating.

"Hey, Stomarek, come here," she said and handed the 18-year-old leftovers from the supervisors' meal. She would do this for him over the next year and a half. When he talks about her today, his eyes light up, and his face breaks into a smile. He laughs when he recalls a man named Joel Zolna, who sat next to him on a train to one of the last camps where he was imprisoned. The train slowed as it curved around a mountain. Isaac was too weak to jump and run, and Joel couldn't flee with his identification numbers painted on his coat. Isaac's coat had the numbers sewn on, so he ripped them off and switched coats with Joel, who jumped off the slowing train and escaped. After the war, Joel would take Isaac out to nightclubs and concerts.

These are things Isaac, who is 90 now, wants to remember. He wants to remember every person who did something to lessen his pain.

"Sparks of holiness," he calls them.

They lit the world in its darkest days.

Yet, some things he can't forget. He can't forget the death and ugliness he saw as he was shipped from camp to camp, nine times. He can't forget the boxcars or the beatings, the stifling heat, the burning cold. He can't forget the cruelty that people showed. He can't forget that they killed his brother, parents, six sisters, grandmother, mentor, aunts, uncles and countless cousins and friends.

The world was full of brutality and misery and stench. But despite it all, those sparks of holiness — they never died.

"Ani ma'amin," he says in Hebrew.

"I believe."

At the back of his house in Champaign, with a corner window overlooking a pleasant pond, is the study where Isaac spends most of his days. It is the study of a scholar: glossy leather armchairs, a wide desk in disarray, 10 columns of built-in shelves holding books with titles such as "Sermons for the Seventies" and "The Rescue of Danish Jewry." His rabbinic diplomas line one wall. He sits on a leather couch facing a TV and a picture of his son, David, shaking President Ronald Reagan's hand. Piers Morgan is on CNN talking about taxes and gay marriage.

Isaac, who moved to Champaign in 1974 to be the rabbi of Sinai Temple, used to have more visitors. He has stopped encouraging them to come. It's so hard to entertain anymore, and he has enough in his house to keep busy. He has his wife, who stops in his study for short conversations and a kiss on the cheek, and a caretaker who answers the phone when he's busy ("Neuman residence") and pours him mineral water or wine.

But most of all, he has his books. He takes them off the shelf as if they are old friends and stacks them on a side table. Reading takes his mind off the aches of his body, more so than whatever the doctor prescribes.

Yes, his body aches. His hands shake. It's funny, when he was 60, he thought he was going to die in his 70s. He figured a human could only endure so much trauma and pain without skimming off a few years. But even after his second coronary bypass surgery at 73, he kept going. Always another birthday. Always another reason to keep living.

He moves to the kitchen for dinner: salad, chicken, peas, rice. He pushes up his sleeves before the meal and says a short prayer over bread. There, on his left forearm, are six numbers in dark ink: 143945. A souvenir from Auschwitz.

He was born in 1922 in Zdunska Wola, a Polish town of about 8,000 Jews living alongside 12,000 Poles and ethnic Germans. For the first 17 years of his life, Itsekel, as he was called, grew up as a pious boy studying Torah, Talmud, Midrash and any other Jewish text he could get his hands on.

His teacher and mentor was Rabbi Mendel, a former soldier in the German army in World War I, legendary in Zdunska Wola for his wisdom.

The rabbi taught Itsekel about Judaism and life. He once told a Talmudic story, one of a second-century rabbi who stopped in the ruins of Jerusalem to pray. Elijah, the mystical Jewish prophet, met him outside and reprimanded him for praying in ruins. The story was supposed to warn readers to stay away from ruins because they might be unsafe. But Rabbi Mendel taught Itsekel his own interpretation. If you stand at the ruins of your civilization, he said, do not dwell.

Your prayer should be short. Be careful, for it is hallowed ground.

Itsekel's family fled Zdunska Wola when the German army invaded in 1939. They were less than 35 miles away when they turned back — escaping to Russia would be too difficult with eight children, they decided. They returned to a shattered world: broken windows, burned factories, ruined homes. Rabbi Mendel had been arrested and executed for studying Torah under the new Nazi rule.

Isaac was sent to his ninth and final concentration camp of the war in Ebensee, Austria, in April 1945, one month before the Americans came. He doesn't remember much about the liberation. He was dying from starvation and tuberculosis. He weighed about 80 pounds. He remembers the Americans setting up hospitals for the former prisoners and putting the new prisoners — the Nazi soldiers — in charge of caring for them.

Isaac was brought back to health by doctors and nurses who had worn swastikas just a few weeks earlier. It was weird. At one point, the doctors sent him to the hospital psychiatrist, a former German officer, because Isaac's hands wouldn't stop shaking. The officer boasted that he had been trained in psychology by a disciple of Sigmund Freud. The Nazi officer, trained by an Austrian Jew. Isaac wasn't sure if the officer realized the irony.

Some of the nurses assured him they had never hurt a Jew during the war. Someone asked: Did you ever care for Jewish patients? Well, no, they said, the Jewish patients never were brought to them. They only did what they were told.

Twenty years later, as a rabbi in Cedar Rapids, Iowa, Isaac wanted to attend Martin Luther King Jr.'s civil rights march in Selma, Ala. The board members of his synagogue tried to convince him not to go. They didn't understand why he should risk his life for black people in the Deep South.

Isaac reflected on his biblical knowledge, his companion since the age of 3. There, in Exodus 12:49, he found words that rang deep inside him, clear as the Ten Commandments: "One law shall be given to you and the stranger who lives among you."

Didn't he know what it was like to be treated like a stranger in his own land? Didn't he know what happened when fear stopped good people from speaking out? He didn't want to be like the nurses at Ebensee, like the silent, good Germans.

He went to Selma.

Sometimes, people ask him: "Where was God?" Where was Isaac's God between 1941 and '45, in Junikowo, St. Martin's, Fuerstenfelde, Auschwitz-Birkenau, Fuenfteichen, Gross-Rosen, Mauthausen, Wels and Ebensee?

What God would give Isaac dreams almost 70 years later about frantically trying to escape from guards and killers? What God would extinguish entire families, generations of memories?

People ask: "Where was God?"

Isaac believes God was in the sparks of holiness that radiated through the darkness, in the people who maintained their humanity in the brutality and misery and stench. There is good and there is evil in the world; that cannot be changed. He believes it is our job — not His — to seek the good and stop the evil.

People ask: "Where was God?"

Isaac asks: "Where was man?"

It is said that during the Holocaust, some Jewish prisoners sang this Hebrew text on the way to death camps: "Ani ma'amin, ani ma'amin b'emunah sh'leimah" — "I believe, I believe, with perfect faith." Sitting on his leather couch, Isaac sings this song in the traditional melody, the one that his congregation at Sinai Temple sings every year on YomHaShoah, the day of remembrance for the Holocaust.

Isaac knows it is hard for those who were not there to remember it well. He knows that the best way to remember is to listen to the stories of witnesses. Yet, so often people only remember the cruelty. Yes, the cruelty must be present in every story, but Isaac wants to warn people: Be careful not to dwell on it. The Holocaust is hallowed ground. It is the ruins of a civilization.

He wants the world to remember it the way he does: Despite the hunger and thirst, brutality and death, ani ma'amin — "I believe."

In the sparks of holiness.

They light the world even in its darkest days.

Emily Siner, from Glenwood, Ill., is a 2013 graduate of the University of Illinois. She began her journalism experience in high school, where she was editor-in-chief of the Homewood-Flossmoor Voyager. In college, she was a food and drink writer for buzz *magazine and the publication's copy chief and online editor. She also became the executive producer of a student-run convergence media project that covered the 2012 presidential election. She has interned at the Southtown Star, the Scripps Howard Foundation Wire, WILL Illinois Public Media and the Los Angeles Times. Her story on Rabbi Isaac Neuman was honored with the journalism department's first-place Marian and Barney Brody Creative Feature Article Writing Award. It was ranked 14th nationally in the Hearst journalism award for personality-profile writing.*

2

The longings of … a beautiful boy

By Christian Gollayan

He's 6 feet tall barefoot, 6-feet-5 in his Jeffrey Campbell heels. He loves Lady Gaga and Andy Warhol and beautiful women who don't care about what other people think. He loves vodka. He takes it straight up, pursing his lips, keeping a composed face. It makes him feel as if he's made of plastic; it's reassuring. If he can keep a strong face after a shot, he can keep a strong face after anything.

His fingers are long and slender like a lady's. His face is soft and angular. His eyes are almond-shaped with long lashes that flutter like butterflies. He loves bubble baths. When he shuts his mouth, his lips don't fully close, giving him a permanent pout. He has skin like porcelain. Wrinkles are his enemies. He has trained his eyebrows not to move when he speaks. He likes having an expression-less face. He doesn't want strangers to know him.

He categorizes his life through his outfits. It depends on how he feels when he wakes up in the morning. Different days he'll feel happy, gothic, angry, butchy, vengeful or hopeful.

One recent Monday he awoke thinking Marilyn Monroe — old Hollywood glamour. He wore his high-waist checkered pants with a tight-fitted turtle neck and finished the ensemble with blood-red lipstick. He tries to stay away from classic-red lipstick. Every girl and gay guy wears that now. It has become the gay male version of a Plain Jane. He wants to be anything but ordinary.

He doesn't want to be a woman. He just doesn't understand why a man can't wear lilac lipstick or velvet nail polish or sequined stilettos to his 9 a.m. class without getting stared at. No matter; he likes it when people look at him; he gets worried when they don't. He likes it when he makes people uncomfortable.

He spent the past few years worrying about what people thought of him, whether they thought his voice was too high or he spoke with his hands too much. No more. Now every morning is a coming-out day.

He likes to use hard descriptions such as "marble eyes" and "leather hair." He loves perfumes, particularly Britney Spears' Midnight Fantasy. He wears it on

A self-portrait by Gino Baileau.

his pretty days. He knows that some men he meets at campus bars would love to take him home for the night but never introduce him to their parents.

He doesn't kiss on the first date. Or the second. Or the third. He was once offered a job as a go-go dancer in Chicago. He turned it down. He's not that type of boy. A 50-something man on Facebook once offered him a weekend of dinners and shopping on Rodeo Drive. He turned the man down. He's not that type of boy, either.

He is an Aquarius. He was born in 1991. A visual person, he doesn't read newspapers and hates politics. They make his head hurt. He loves magazines because he can look at pretty pictures and not have to read anything.

He came to the University of Illinois as an art education major but soon realized he wanted to do photography. He is now a junior. His photographs for his classes contain thin 20-something models airbrushed to look like mannequins, like plastic. He hopes someday to see his work in V, Harper's Bazaar or W with his name emblazoned on the corner of the page: Photographs by Gino Baileau.

That is his artist name. He started using that name when he became a photographer. He doesn't like his real name, Gino Gusich. He hates the alliteration, the GG. He likes Baileau better. It means "beautiful boy" in Italian.

His mother and his grandmother called him that since he was a baby. He loves his mother more than anything.

Gusich. It reminds him of his childhood in Melrose Park, that small, Italian community, a 20-minute car ride west of Chicago. Gino calls it the ghetto. He was raised in a house full of women: his two older sisters, mother and grandmother. The walls of his bedroom were covered with Britney Spears posters. He loved playing with his sisters' Barbies. Gino's parents separated when he was 5. His father was a Weekend Dad.

Gino was an ugly baby. His mother told him that he looked like a newborn alien because of his oversized head. Every day after preschool, he'd cry if his grandmother didn't feed him two double-decker sandwiches. By middle school, he was overweight. His mother put him on a low-carb diet. By eighth grade, he was average sized. By high school, he was thin.

Gino Baileau doesn't want people to see his grade school pictures. He is not that person anymore. He is now thin and angular and beautiful. Now, he tries to eat two meals a day. He admits he doesn't have a healthy diet. Today, he had a can of Progresso soup, 60 calories.

Gino is wearing black H&M harem pants, 5-inch leather wedges and a red vintage blazer with a studded belt around his waist. He's wearing black lipstick from MAC called Dark Night. His hair is wrapped in a black infinity scarf, and he's wearing thick, rhinestone sunglasses. He just came back from his photography class. He woke up today feeling vengeful.

Lately, Gino's been thinking about the people in his childhood who did him wrong. He says that kids in his grade school sold weed and ecstasy in the bathrooms. He remembers times he was threatened with assault in the boy's bathroom or on his way home. He was an easy target, after all: that chubby boy who hung out only with the girls, talked with his hands, and who knew all the lyrics to every Britney Spears song.

He remembers a classmate in fourth grade who would find every opportunity to harass Gino, calling him "faggot" or "fat boy." One day, after school, Gino's mother asked if anything was bothering him. His mother always knew how he felt. He said, no, he was fine. Later, Gino overheard his mother on the phone with his father. His mother was asking him what she should do. Gino would never forget the advice his mother relayed from his father: Let Gino take care of it. Let him man up. Don't let him be a wuss.

One day, during lunch, the classmate came up to Gino with that smirk on his face, Diet Coke in hand. Gino remembers the boy calling him a name. Something triggered inside Gino. He leaped from his seat and grabbed the boy by the neck and pushed him to the ground. Then Gino remembers taking the boy's Diet Coke and sipping from it.

To Gino, being gay is bravery. It's a liberation of many things. Of sex. Of the way you act. Of fashion. He is an extremist, and if he says he's gonna be gay, he's gonna be gay all the way, which is why he wears what he wears to class, to the mall and to the bars.

He began dressing this way only nine months ago. In his mother's house, he'd lose himself in the fashion blogs of Alexander McQueen, Terry Richardson and Marc Jacobs. He'd sneak into his mother's and sisters' makeup boxes and experiment with different looks. He loved how he could use pencils to elongate his eyebrows, how blush could highlight his cheekbones.

Gino never had a coming-out moment with his mother or sisters. They always knew. At first, his father said that Gino could be gay and still dress like a man. Gino then took his sister's softball shin guards, embellished them with metal spikes, connected them with chains and wore the ensemble as shoulder pads. Gino remembers asking his father if he now looked like a man.

His father eventually came around to accepting him.

On Gino's right index finger is a tattoo, in cursive — "liberate." His right hand is often adorned in accessories. He sometimes wears his sister's armadillo ring or spiked bracelets or his gold-plated bangle (he calls it his Wonder Woman cuff). They are his weapons. He never knows when he might need to use them, especially at the bars.

When Gino walks into a bar, it's a spectacle. People he never knew come up to him and tell him how they love his fashion sense or how he's beautiful. Strangers take pictures of him. He loves the attention.

One night, though, at Fire Station, a tall man by the bar looked at Gino a certain way. Gino paid no mind until one of his friends pointed the man out. Gino looked at the man, who made a gun of his hand and pointed to his head, pretending to shoot himself. Gino, in his nude-laced button-up shirt and fur stole that wrapped around his shoulders like a cape, made his way toward the man and asked what his problem was. The man called him a "devil" or a "demon;" the memories of Gino and his friends differ.

Gino believes men like that don't expect men who wear lipstick or high heels or skin-tight jeans to stick up for themselves. Men like that expect them to just take it, maybe roll their eyes and sit back down like a lady.

Gino is not like other men, or ladies. He remembers looking at his hand, the same hand that had "liberate" tattooed on it. On his ring finger was his grandfather's diamond horseshoe ring. Gino looked back at the man — and then punched him. Gino doesn't remember much of anything else. He says the man came out of it with a horseshoe-stamped forehead. Gino walked away with two broken nails.

Gino wonders if he will ever find a man who will love him for who he is. He is now getting ready in his apartment for another night out in Champaign, deciding what to wear. His bedroom is on a high floor overlooking the north side of Green Street. He is humming along to one of his favorite songs, Cyndi Lauper's "Girls Just Want to Have Fun." Tonight, he decides to wear a leopard-print blazer with ripped jeans and leather wedges.

Gino's only been in one serious relationship, with a man who didn't like how he dressed or his aspiration to be a famous fashion photographer. He gave Gino an ultimatum: Dress differently and choose a different career, or their relationship was over. Gino left him. After all, his favorite quote is from a Lauper song, which is now ringing through his room:

Some boys take a beautiful girl
And hide her away from the rest of the world
I want to be the one to walk in the sun
Oh girls they want to have fun

Gino can't imagine growing old. He is 21, in the first blossom of adulthood, his heels now planted on the ground, wide-eyed and hopeful. Maybe he'll make it as a high-fashion photographer in Chicago or L.A. or New York. Maybe he'll get to work for Marc Jacobs or W or Sarah Burton. Maybe. Who knows what's in the future?

He slips into his heeled wedges. In a couple of hours, he will be at Red Lion, dancing on tables, being photographed by strangers, being told he is beautiful. And he will smile and say thank you and lose himself on the dance floor, what's ahead of him a mystery.

Christian Gollayan is from Manila, Philippines, and a 2013 graduate in news-editorial journalism at the University of Illinois. He was a staff writer for buzz *magazine and* The Daily Illini *and the editor-in-chief of IMPULSE magazine. He also worked as a news intern at the University of Illinois News Bureau and was an editorial intern for DETAILS Magazine. He is now a freelance writer in New York City.*

3

Charlie's rocking chair

By Aske Denning

From morning to late afternoon, Monday through Saturday, Charlie Sweitzer works in his shop, next to his home on West John Street in Champaign. He is 78 or 77 ... no, 78 years old. This morning, he is ready to begin crafting a wooden rocking chair. Its distinctive back will be made of four bowed slats of bird's eye maple. The wood's name derives from the lumber's thousands of tiny, spiraling eyes, a pattern that makes the maple surface look like a map of a hilly landscape. Charlie is a little nervous about building the chair because the client living in the country outside Mattoon is a fellow craftsman Charlie admires.

"He's such a fine woodworker, so I'm very hesitant."

Almost a decade ago, Charlie and his son, John, founded the Sweitzer & Sweitzer furniture shop. They sell handmade furniture inspired by the Shakers, a Protestant sect that emigrated from England to America in 1774. The Shakers did not believe in ornamenting their furniture. Utility was seen as the highest worship of God. Although a Sweitzer piece can take weeks of labor, the men's creations are spare, clean and functional — honest, Charlie calls them.

"You can see how it is put together," he says.

Charlie, a tall, lean man with large, knuckled hands and a white, bushy beard, came late to making chairs. For more than 20 years, he worked as a pastor with the McKinley Foundation. He retired in 1996 believing his work lacked a feeling of tangibility, of results. That's when he took up chair-making.

It began with a present. Charlie was still with McKinley and on his birthday — who knows which one? — John gave him *The Book of Shaker Furniture*. John was already building furniture. Charlie had no idea why the hell his son had given him the book, but he was dissatisfied at work and so he decided to give chair-making a try.

He bought tools and attended workshops in Michigan and England. The book that was a birthday present from his son became Charlie's new Bible. Because Sweitzer & Sweitzer is a family business, people tend to think that the craft was

Photo by Darrell Hoemann/The News-Gazette

SLICES OF LIFE
12

handed down from father to son.

"Wrong," Charlie says.

In his first attempt at building a chair, Charlie drilled the angles incorrectly. "Then there's nothing you can do, except cut up the pieces and burn 'em."

But with time, Charlie learned the lessons of craftsmanship from his son: patience and dogged attention to detail.

"He knows a lot about furniture," Charlie says of John.

The Sweitzers' shop today consists of three rooms, two for working and one for storage, as well as an attic that is stacked with raw lumber: white oak, maple, cherry, hickory and walnut.

Sounds of the shop: A mallet knocking the arm of a chair in place, the sharp metallic whirl of a table saw, an old sawdust-covered stereo playing the Chatham Baroque ensemble or the Argentinean guitarist Gustavo Santaolalla. The shop's dusty air is dry to the throat, yet fresh from the scent of wood being cut, sanded and chiseled. Above the entrance, tilting to the left, hangs a wooden sign: SWEITZER & SWEITZER.

Besides the bird's eye maple back slats, Charlie's rocking chair will be made of cherry wood uprights, legs, stretchers, arms, rockers and a shawl rail, the top bar on which the Shakers would hang their garments.

Cherry is not as strong as, say, hickory or oak. But what it lacks in hardiness it makes up for in elegance. In its light-colored body run very fine, curved lines of grain. As the wood oxidizes, it develops a deep rose-colored patina.

By now, Charlie has built several hundred chairs, and from time to time, he builds a chair he admires. In such a chair, the joints fit tightly and cleanly, and Charlie has made the right selections in back slats and uprights so that the grain patterns flow elegantly.

This morning, after having drilled holes in the rocker's front legs, Charlie marks the back legs with a pencil to indicate where he will be mortising — drilling rectangular holes to hold the maple slats, which will be placed between the two back posts like steps on a ladder.

Chairs are a headache because their pieces meet at so many varying angles. Some angles are right, some are 15 degrees, others are 10, no, let's see ... 8 degrees! Charlie measures them all by hand, the old-fashioned way.

When Charlie began chair-making, John was worried that sharing his shop would not work out. He knew Charlie was unhappy at his job, and John did not want his father's distress to infect the shop. But Charlie mellowed out immediately.

"We're actually able to get along," says Charlie, who gladly lets his son's work take priority over his own when the shop is busy. "But it has become very clear to me, as an indentured servant, that the only way I'm gonna get outta this shop is when I die."

With that, he laughs.

Charlie pulls out two sets of back slats. Four maple slats in each set, firmly fixed in frames meant to keep them bowed until assembly. He carefully assesses each set. Not just the grain of the individual slats and their amount of eye, but how nature's designs in the four pieces interplay with each other.

"I don't know," he mumbles as the sound of Santaolalla's melancholic charango fills the air. "I think I'll choose this set."

Charlie can't really explain. In the end, it is simply intuition. Next, Charlie sands the slats — first with a power sander, then sand paper by hand. The final detailed sanding could be done in the dark because, at this stage, Charlie sees any roughness with his fingers, not his eyes. He measures the angle of the slats, writes "18 degrees" on a piece of blue reminder-tape, and moves down to his next step.

"I don't trust my memory," he says and checks a document of procedures an extra time before drilling four rectangular slits in each of the chair's back legs.

For cutting mortises, Charlie uses a machine built by a funny old duck of a woodworker in Wisconsin. "He builds 'em one at a time."

The mortising machine cuts are rounded, so Charlie needs to square their ends by hand. From a drawer stuffed with tools, he pulls out a set of chisels. His favorite is Japanese and formed like a fishtail. The chiseling makes muffled, crunching sounds as Charlie works the shape of his mortises.

Then something happens. Despite being fastened to the table by a clamp, one of the legs moves a touch as Charlie chisels it, and an edge of one the mortises goes a little off square. Charlie is not happy.

"This might be a throwaway piece. But we'll see."

Charlie didn't used to be so fussy. Working every day with John, who helps correct his father's mistakes, has made Charlie a perfectionist, which he never was. He is surprised. He used to believe he was too old to learn anything new.

"Alright, now we're gonna fit these babies," he says to himself.

Making the back slats fit into the mortises of the uprights is a matter of trial and error. Charlie eventually gets to the mortise with the off-square line.

"Is that gonna work?" his son asks.

Charlie sands the end of the slat again and again and patiently attempts to press it into the slit, hoping to feel that perfect, tight fit.

"I think I can make it work," Charlie says and sands again, blows away the dust, goes to assemble.

"Shall we pray?" the former pastor asks.

It fits.

These are not the golden years for Charlie; they are the forgetful and clumsy years. He sometimes forgets where he put his tools and his hands shake a little when they are idle. His body does not allow him to lift heavy pieces anymore. He has had to cut down on the number of art fairs he attends with John. Yet Charlie considers his life privileged.

"I walk 10 yards to work. I work with John at least five days a week." Charlie breaks into a warm smile. "He's so kind. I'm among the lucky."

On a wall in the shop hangs a framed quote from Thomas Merton, an American mystic and Trappist monk: "Build a chair as if an angel was going to sit in it."

It has been two weeks since Charlie began crafting his rocking chair. Its body stands assembled in the Sweitzer shop. The remaining process will include adding a seat of jute fibre and interwoven green and burnt orange Shaker tape of cotton. Because Charlie wants this chair to be something special, he will apply six layers of finish, rather than the usual three or four.

"It came out OK," Charlie says as he takes a careful look at his work: a classic, a potential heirloom. He smiles.

"I think I'll be happy with it."

Born in Denmark, Aske Denning had no idea what he wanted to do after graduating college with a degree in international business and English. But he knew he could write, and he knew that he wanted to travel to America. While taking classes at the Danish School of Media and Journalism, Aske applied for a Fulbright grant that would allow him to study journalism in the United States. He received the grant in 2012 and enrolled in the University of Illinois journalism graduate program. His story on furniture maker Charlie Sweitzer was his first step into the world of "intimate journalism" — a world he does not intend to leave. Aske worked as a multimedia reporter for the Daily Illini. In summer 2013, he moved to South Bronx, N.Y., to report for his journalism master's project. He currently lives, blogs and reports in Copenhagen, hoping to make a career in feature and nonfiction writing.

Photo by Darrell Hoemann/The News-Gazette

4

Can these bones live?

By Robert Holly

Bishop Morris Paul Lockett sits patiently in the former crack house at 205 E. Garwood St., in Champaign, waiting for his congregation to arrive. It's a cold, gray winter afternoon. But inside, The New House of Prayer Church is warm and bright, as soft light filters through colorful, thin drapes.

Lockett waits with his suit coat unbuttoned and his clerical collar stretched tight around his thick neck. He reads his Bible from the front row of wooden pews, rehearsing the day's sermon with his sister and his wife. Today, he will preach from Ezekiel 37: "The valley of dry bones." His goal is to tell his parishioners that, no matter how bleak a situation appears, there is always hope as long as you maintain faith. He quickly goes over the story one more time, though he knows it well:

The hand of the Lord was on me, and he brought me out by the Spirit of the Lord and set me in the middle of a valley; it was full of bones. He led me back and forth among them, and I saw a great many bones on the floor of the valley, bones that were very dry. He asked me, "Son of man, can these bones live?"

Lockett, no longer a young man at age 61, has been forced to confront a similar question. The New House of Prayer is in Bristol Park, a troubled 144-acre neighborhood less than a mile north of downtown Champaign. Most of the homes in the neighborhood are dilapidated and valued significantly lower than comparable homes nearby. Many of them, Lockett says, aren't suitable for people to live in. The neighborhood is also a haven for criminals. In 2011, the city concluded: "Since 2000, the area has reported a variety of crime including domestic battery, assault and murder. Surveys of the neighborhood during this time period also confirm the presence of drug sales, prostitution and robbery."

Lockett is not surprised. During a period when the church was abandoned, crack heads used it as a stop-off house to get high. He resurrected the church in

1999, throwing away crack paraphernalia scattered on the church's floor. But still, crack heads kept hiding drugs between the deteriorating planks of the church's facade, hoping police wouldn't search inside its holy, paint-peeled walls.

The city has decided the best way to end the neighborhood's rampant poverty, violence and drug use is to demolish it and rebuild. The only building that will be spared is the Family Dollar. As part of the redevelopment project, Lockett's church — which has been tied to his family since his grandmother, Elnora McKinney, presided as its pastor more than 40 years ago — will be "relocated." His church will be destroyed.

Lockett wonders: Can The New House of Prayer survive?

Shortly after 1 p.m., his nondenominational flock begins to arrive. The woman who says she used to be homeless, and the man who says he wants to become a cop. The teenager wearing his Sunday suit and a flat-brimmed hat. The girl with pink butterfly clips in her hair, and the little boy eating Cheetos. He sits next to another child more interested in his Gameboy than church.

Parishioners enter Lockett's little white-painted church with the bent cross in its front yard until the congregation grows to about 30 people. Bishop Lockett stands and ambles to the pulpit. After cleaning his silver-framed glasses, he preaches into the microphone.

"I would like to use as a subject today, if you're with me here, 'when the wind blows.'" The old amplifier connected to his microphone crackles, and his voice sticks and clings like sandpaper rubbing against wet hands. "When the wind blows, different things happen. But there's something about God's wind, God's anointments, God's blessings — God's spiritual blowing of the wind. Oh, something happens when God begins to blow."

Preaching comes naturally to Lockett. He has known he wanted to preach since he was 17 years old and living with his grandmother. One night, he had a dream. He was in a white robe preaching. When he awoke, he was startled to find himself actually preaching in bed. To make a living, Lockett has been a Walmart greeter, a mall security guard and a nursing assistant. But, since that night, he has always preached.

The congregation replies to their pastor with a chorus of "Yes, Lord," "Amen," and "That's right."

Sister Bonnie Smith, who recently joined the church along with her two young children, backs her pastor up by keeping a crude rhythm on a drum set in the corner. Lockett's sister, Pat, holds a tambourine, ready to assist any of the parishioners brave enough to stand up for God. A woman sitting toward the back of the church, joined by her small children, soon does.

"I just want to thank God for waking me up, and keeping me and my family going another day," she tells the church, her voice choked with emotion. "I get jealous sometimes. I feel like I've been working so hard, I should have the things that everybody else has. But God's been making a way. I got to keep my faith, and keep holding on to my head, and keep helping others."

Suddenly, she begins to sing: "Because of who you are, I give you glory. Because of who you are I give you praise —" Unlike Smith's rough drum rhythm, her voice is beautiful and smooth. Close your eyes, and you'd think she was a young diva on the radio instead of a young mother converting her woes into song in a homely church set for destruction. Without opening any hymnal, the rest of the church joins in singing, too.

"I worship you because of who you are ..."

Then, a young man with long, braided hair stands. He thanks God for letting him see another day and apologizes for being absent from the church recently. He has wanted to be there. He really has. Abrupt tears flow down his face and he has a difficult time speaking. The other churchgoers encourage him: "Take your time," and "That's all right." The young man tells them he has been busy working. He has had to take care of his family. He starts to say something else, but his words are inaudible. He stands nakedly, sniffling and crying so hard his shoulders shake.

A parishioner comes to the rescue. Again, without any prompt, a woman erupts in song and the entire church follows: "You don't have to worry, and don't you be afraid. Joy comes in the morning, for troubles they don't last always. There's a friend in Jesus, who will wipe your tears away —"

As Lockett starts to preach again, his voice grows louder, and sweat glistens on his forehead. His eyes look up from Ezekiel 37 and scan the room. His demeanor demands his parishioners' attention. To his right is a hole left by a stray bullet fired through his church's faux stained-glass window last year. It was a Saturday. The window is decorated in a floral pattern with swatches of red, blue and yellow. Cracks have spread around the hole, spider-webbing throughout the pane. After the bullet burst through the window, it burrowed into a wall next to the pulpit. It is a constant reminder of the neighborhood's hard reality.

Soon, Champaign will send appraisers to assess the value of Lockett's church. In theory, he will receive the determined value and be able to buy another with funds given to him by the city. It's up to Lockett to find the building that will be his new New House of Prayer. A city official described the process as akin to trading in a used car for money to buy a new one. Once Lockett has bought another church, the city will even pay him for "startup costs," such as advertising expenses or moving fees.

Yet Lockett worries: If the properties in Bristol Park are valued significantly below comparable properties, how will he buy a similar church somewhere else? And, besides, he doesn't want to move his church somewhere else. Bristol Park may be infested with drugs and violence, but he believes that's the perfect place for his church. That way, he can help. Many of the people in Bristol Park don't go to his church, Lockett says, but they respect it. Sometimes, they depend on it.

Consider the sobbing woman who came by the church on New Year's Eve wearing only her pajamas as Lockett and New House of Prayer members were having a watch party. She had been diagnosed with cancer and wanted to pray.

Or the anonymous girl who left a $10 bill and a handwritten letter for Bishop Lockett on the Church's door: "This is the only money I have left to my name. We really need other things for our house that I could spend it on but I think it is more important to give it to god. So if you could Please pray for our family — pray for my sister, my brother, nephews, nieces, my dad." She signed the letter "God's Child." Lockett kept the letter, which he has laminated.

Bishop Lockett concludes the service by asking for donations. A girl carries a gold plate from person to person. Few offer nothing, and it quickly fills with silver spare change and crumpled singles. Most of the money will be used to pay the church's utility bills.

When Lockett finishes his service, he is sweaty and exhausted. He mops his face with a cloth and plops down on a couch near the pulpit. The adults trickle out the church's side door. Outside in the cold, the children play in the snow.

For now, Lockett and The New House of Prayer have time. Until the city acquires all the property in the rehabilitation area — a total of 90 parcels — he won't have to move. City officials say they'll be flexible and work with Lockett. But whether it all takes months or a year, this is certain: Lockett will have to move, and his grandmother's New House of Prayer will physically be no more.

Lockett says he supports the city's decision to start over. He understands the neighborhood's pain. Before Lockett had a church, he preached on Champaign's streets. His favorite spot was at the corner of Market Street and Bradley Avenue. If he can't find a new building, maybe, he says, he'll return to that busy intersection. Or maybe he'll invite his congregation to Ehlers trailer park and into his own small living room.

"I'll do that if I have to. It's not going to stop us."

Because The New House of Prayer is more than a building to Lockett. His church is the young man with the braids who cries nakedly before him. It's Sister Bonnie Smith banging on the drums, and his sister, Pat, gripping the tambourine. It's offering support for a neighbor battling cancer. It's an anonymous letter and children playing in the snow.

These are the bones Bishop Lockett thinks about.
They are the bones he believes must live.

A Lisle, Ill., native, Robert Holly first figured out he was interested in journalism at Downers Grove North High School, where he served as graphics editor and managing editor for its school paper, The Omega. After high school, he went to the University of Illinois and graduated in 2012 with a bachelor's degree in advertising. His interest in journalism was rekindled senior year when he took Walt Harrington's Great Books of Journalism class. He refocused on journalism and successfully applied to the university's master's degree program. During that yearlong program, he worked as a reporter for the online newsroom, CU-CitizenAccess.org, and contributed material to The News-Gazette. He graduated with his master's degree in journalism in August 2013. He plans on telling stories like this one for the rest of his life.

Photo by Darrell Hoemann/The News-Gazette

5

Life among the laundry

By Marisa Gwidt

"Oh, boy," Charlie High sighs as he watches a college student drag in four heaping bags of laundry. "She won't finish in time."

It's 9:50 on a Monday night at Starcrest Cleaners in Champaign. Charlie's supposed to lock the doors at 11. Yet here is this young woman, opening a silver front-loader and preparing to toss in a load of darks. Charlie, 67 years old, hobbles over in cuffed, faded jeans and intervenes.

"Uh-uh," he mutters to the student, shaking his head as though she were about to make a grave mistake. "I recommend that one," he says, pointing to another washer outwardly identical.

"Really? What makes that one superior?" she inquires with a smile, already starting to inch over in its direction.

The question clearly takes Charlie aback. His customers rarely engage him — the Monday-through-Friday janitor — in conversation. Charlie removes his navy blue Sturgis biker hat and thoughtfully smoothes his thin gray hair with stout, pale fingers. He then replaces his hat and leans his short, heavy-set frame against the recommended washer.

"It spins quicker," he explains, pleased to talk laundry physics with someone. "It's never got a service tag on it, and the coins don't jam."

All evening, as he talks, Charlie keeps working — wiping, mopping, sweeping.

"I needed to keep busy, and this place is always busy," he says as he stops sweeping to pick up a piece of pink lint a woman dropped right in front of him. "Hurt too much to think 'bout her not bein' at home."

"Her" was Charlie's wife, Janet, of 36 years. She died of colon cancer in 2003. After Janet died, Charlie went on Social Security. But money was tight, and so he took a job at the laundromat.

"Even if I had money, I would've kept workin'," he said. "Thinkin' 'bout her all the time would've killed me. Nobody knows how hard it is."

Charlie had never imagined illness could destroy such a beautiful, caring woman.

"She'd grocery shop for widow ladies in town," he remembers, teary eyed. "It isn't fair she's gone. I don't show it, but I still got a lot of anger in me over the whole mess."

Charlie makes his rounds at the laundromat. He empties the trash, ensures that the 75-cent Tide boxes are stacked neatly in their wall dispenser and wipes the blue droplets of detergent off the machines. From the corner of his eye, he notices that a washing machine has stolen a quarter from the student with the four laundry bags. He walks over to her and takes a quarter out of his pocket. He has already forgiven her for bringing in so much laundry at the last minute.

"Ya need dryer sheets?" he asks, shifting from foot to foot. "People're always leavin' dryer sheets. They're Bounce, not the cheap stuff."

Long before his nights were filled with the hum of dryers and smell of detergents, Charlie was a little boy living in Indianola, Ill. — a tiny town about 40 miles southeast of Champaign. Janet lived 15 miles away in Broadlands. They went to different schools and met only briefly in the spring of 1963.

"We met for a second at a school baseball game. Guess she remembered me, 'cause when I went to the Army, she asked Mom for my address."

While Charlie was stationed in Oahu, Hawaii, as a tank repairman, Janet wrote him several times a week. He became so excited to receive her letters that he'd be in the camp's main lobby at 4:10 p.m. when the mail carrier arrived each day. Sometimes, he'd even get a care package.

"I liked her raisin oatmeal cookies," he says, smiling. "I didn't leave those things layin' around. The other soldiers would raid me if I did."

Charlie disappears into the laundromat's back room to fetch a dryer sheet. He reappears and hands it to the student in a pleased manner.

"Thank you," she says politely. When Charlie leaves her alone at the washer, she sniffs the dryer sheet. It's scentless, stiffer than it should be, old, and she discreetly slips it into a nearby trash can.

Charlie got out of the Army when he was 21. After a long boat ride and two flights, he sat down for a nice dinner with his parents.

"I don't know what I ate 'cause I was thinkin' about Janet the whole time," he says, as he fills a bucket with mopping solution. "I borrowed Dad's car and drove to see her."

That night, more than three years after they had met, the young couple went on their first date. They visited a hamburger joint and ordered root beer floats. They were married four months later.

When Charlie's on duty at the laundromat, he will help an old woman start a washer. He will recommend the best-sized dryer for a man with an oversized load. He will remind a mother to wash her white bathrobe separate from her darks, asking, "Ya don't want that pink, do ya?"

Charlie's customers often roll their eyes in reply. Despite Charlie's slow movements, he's alive in the laundromat. He doesn't mind working. He has worked all his life, mostly as a repairman and janitor.

He also likes his little laundry society. He knows all his regulars and has given most of them nicknames: "Ammonia Man" (a guy who washes all his clothes in straight ammonia), "M&M Girl" (a child Charlie gives packages of M&Ms when she comes in with her dad), and "Bike Couple" (a husband and wife who rig their bikes with special laundry-carrying baskets).

Charlie looks at the student with the four bags of laundry. He dubs her "Allergy Girl" after he learns she's washing everything in her apartment because her doctors are worried about her recurring eye infections.

"I get some crazies here," he says, laughing. "It sure keeps things interesting."

Charlie and Janet were as happy as two poor people could be. They quickly had two sons and started building a garage and house in the small town of Longview, about 25 miles southeast of Champaign. They ran out of money, though, and never built the house. For the next 30 years, they lived in the finished two-car garage.

"Believe it or not, we got two bedrooms in there," Charlie says proudly. They raised two boys in those two bedrooms. "Janet liked it because it was small and easy to keep clean."

In what little free time they had between jobs, they spruced up the house, tended their "lot-and-a-half" lawn and spent time with their boys. Janet worked as a beautician and was a social butterfly, always cheerful. She liked to keep moving, even in her spare time. She got Charlie contributing to the community: grocery shopping for elderly folks, helping them with odd jobs around their homes, mowing their lawns. He liked to help but, mostly, he liked tagging along with Janet.

"We didn't do nothin' big," Charlie says, stopping mid-mop stroke. "We just liked bein' together. It was a real good life."

It's 10:50 in the laundromat. Charlie's chores are done and most of his customers have left. He opens a bottle of Diet Coke, sits on a table and notices the time remaining on Allergy Girl's dryer: 12 minutes. Charlie knows she'll then have to empty the load and possibly even fold it before she leaves and he turns out the lights. He doesn't care. Allergy Girl says she's sorry for taking so long.

"Hey," he replies with a shrug and a gentle smile, "you do what you gotta do."

Charlie's 36 years with Janet went too fast. When she got home from work one day, she sat at the kitchen table and told Charlie she didn't feel right. A week later, doctors told them she'd likely be dead in six months. She seemed fine for the first few months, tolerating the chemotherapy and radiation well.

"It went to her brain is what it did," Charlie whispers. "Near the end, she couldn't do anything for herself."

For the last three weeks of her life, Janet was put into a nursing home. Charlie visited her every day. On the last day of her life, she didn't remember anything.

"Who are you?" she asked him. The question still haunts him.

Clothes stop rotating.

It's 11:02 and Allergy Girl quickly stows her clean laundry in her four bags and heads toward the door. She stops to say good night to Charlie and tells him she'll be back soon.

"You be careful," Charlie says, pointing a finger at her. He directs those same words at most of his customers. It's his catchphrase — the expression of a man who seems to care more about his customers than they care about him. Allergy Girl smiles, giggles and exits. Charlie locks the glass door and "spot mops" the floor one last time.

"I miss her," he says of Janet, "but I find ways to pass the time."

JAM News was the name of the community newsletter Marisa Gwidt founded when she was 11 years old. She and her friends would bike around Plover, Wis., gathering information about neighborhood safety, dog-walking etiquette and babysitting service. In 2012, Marisa graduated from the University of Illinois master's program in journalism. She has written for several student and professional publications, worked in foreign countries and taught journalism to middle schoolers. Currently, Marisa is freelancing in Denver. She lives there with her husband and the Romanian cat she adopted during her service in the Peace Corps.

6

Reborn in America

By Zina Bhaia

So many lights!

I knew that America would be big, but as I looked out my Royal Jordanian Airline window at the sprawling nightscape of Chicago and the towering city-scape of its downtown, I thought, "Oh, my God, it is huge. And Lake Michigan, why do they call it a lake? It is like an ocean." I had flown into Baghdad at night many times, and Baghdad was but a speck of light compared to this glaring city below me.

"What am I getting myself into?" I thought. "I will never find my way around."

My unlikely journey to America had begun nearly a year earlier. As a 28-year-old woman working in the United Nations human rights office in the Green Zone and living with my father and mother in a Shia and Christian neighborhood in central Baghdad, I had seen too much in the four years since Saddam Hussein's fall began: The terrible U.S. bombing; my looting neighbors stealing computer monitors, believing they were TV sets; people giving cookies and tea to the U.S. troops as the tanks bellowed past. Then came the car bombs; the bloody bodies in the streets; my Shia family being driven out of our mostly Sunni neighborhood and our house stripped bare of even its windows; the kidnappings for retaliation or terror or ransom, even my own beautiful, happy, spoiled 16-year-old brother — kidnapped and never seen again, breaking my parents' hearts forever.

I had graduated from Baghdad University in 2002 with an English-language degree and had been hired to translate English movies into Arabic, supposedly for Iraqi TV audiences, but really for Saddam's son, Oday, a crazy man I fortu-nately never met. After the American invasion, I worked for a French organiza-tion distributing artificial legs to Iraqis maimed in the war. My spine was curved badly from having had polio as an infant, and, for the first time in my life, walking with crutches actually helped me get that job. I eventually landed my U.N. job working to expand government services for Iraqis with disabilities, literally a

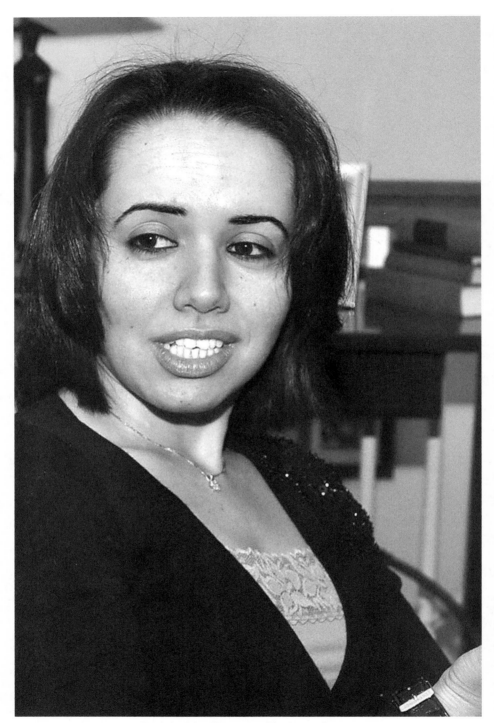

Photo by Darrell Hoemann/The News-Gazette

foreign idea in my country, where people with birth defects are routinely abandoned, ignored and mistreated.

On the side, I volunteered at Al-Mahaba radio, a new Baghdad station self-described as "the voice of Iraqi women." This, too, was a foreign idea in my country, where speaking out for more rights, education, influence, freedom and independence can get a woman harassed, hurt or even killed. Yet that is what we did every day for 16 hours — interviewing the few Iraqi women with high positions in government or business, discussing the substantial rights of women in other countries, taking women's call-in comments about their abusive husbands, brothers and fathers, lobbying for better government benefits for widows, interviewing lawyers and judges to teach women about their legal right to divorce or protection when they are mistreated by the men in their lives.

Al-Mahaba was not loved by everyone, particularly conservative Islamic men. Death threats came by phone. Extreme religious conservatives who did not like our broadcasts got our fuel allotment cut. Government agencies repeatedly denied our grant requests, and the station lived hand-to-mouth on small donations.

Yet it was Al-Mahaba that brought me to Illinois.

When the fledgling station's broadcast tower was destroyed by a car bomb, one of our founders, Bushra Jamil, a 59-year-old Iraqi schoolteacher with a master's degree in biology, traveled to the United States to raise money for a new tower. While on the visit, she was interviewed for National Public Radio's "Morning Edition" and told Al-Mahaba's story. Way off in Urbana, a University of Illinois journalism professor, Lynn Holley, was touched by our tale. She collected money from her faculty colleagues, bought two laptop computers and several digital tape recorders, and shipped them to us.

So when Ms. Bushra, as I called her, passed through Professor Holley's central Illinois town, she stopped to thank her and met Walt Harrington, then head of the UI's Department of Journalism. Before Ms. Bushra was done describing the woes of our free-thinking, iconoclastic radio station, Professor Harrington was brushing away tears and offered on the spot to have his department fund one of our station's aspiring journalists to earn a journalism master's degree at Illinois.

It took a year and more red tape than even we in Iraq — who are, believe me, used to red tape — could imagine. Yet finally, there I was, landing at O'Hare International Airport, as that aspiring Iraqi journalist.

I was an Iraqi woman traveling without a brother, father or husband, something forbidden by Islamic law. I was nervous about what awaited me. But, truthfully, I was thrilled. I had always been fascinated by American life. I had eagerly

watched the TV shows and movies that the Saddam regime allowed on the air —
"Full House," "Boston Public," "Remington Steele," "Titanic," "Braveheart" and
"Lord of the Rings," which I had personally translated in my work for Oday.

What a place America was in my mind!

"Cities, tall buildings, busy people saying whatever they want," I thought.

In America, I believed, no one was discriminated against because of their
thoughts or ideas. And the women — like Laura in "Remington Steele" — were
strong, as strong as American men, not like in Iraq, where women are treated
like cattle, always a man's property, always the shadow of a man. Most important
to me, though, was that in America and all the Western world, people like me —
people with scoliosis, or amputees, blind and deaf people, those with a stutter,
people in wheelchairs — are treated well. In Iraq, they are called names, locked
away in institutions, left to rot in their families' homes. No special buses, no el-
evators, often not even crutches, certainly no decent medical care.

"People in America will not stare at me on the street," I thought.

This I knew from watching Daniel Day-Lewis in "My Left Foot."

I had so many ideas about America, all of them taking their meaning from
my ideas about my own country, ideas that my father — a traditional Muslim man
— often warned me against. I complained about our government's terrible cor-
ruption, about people blindly taking orders from religious leaders without thinking for themselves.

"How ignorant!" I cried.

"Don't talk in public," my father told me again and again. "You are going to
get killed."

My journey's first good sign: At O'Hare airport, a polite man in a uniform
met me with a wheelchair. What shock! I don't believe Baghdad Airport even has
a wheelchair, much less someone to push it for you. At International Terminal
5, Professor Holley was waiting for me, along with Falaah Falih, a 36-year-old
Iraqi-American research scientist at Honeywell outside Chicago, a man I had met
online at "iraq4u," a website connecting Iraqis around the world. I did not know
then that meeting Professor Holley and Falaah, whom I nicknamed "My Angel,"
would change my life forever.

"Hi, finally you are here," said Professor Holley. "Welcome."

She was blond and beautiful, smiling — and then she hugged me, a warm,
strong hug.

"This woman is a professor?" I thought. "This woman with a nice heart?"

In Iraq, professors are somber and formal, even mean. They would never
be friendly toward a student, much less hug you. I didn't know what to call Lynn
Holley — Professor or Ms. Holley or Lynn, so I didn't call her anything. I just

said, "Thank you for being here."

Falaah helped us pack my bags in the car, gave me a cell phone and said goodbye until I would get a chance to visit him in Chicago to tour the city.

My next American surprise was the drive to Champaign. Flat, empty land rolled off in every direction. No tall buildings, no lights, no people, not even animals. And no bombed-out cars, no military Humvees or cement walls or police checkpoints. Only one police car the whole way — and it had stopped someone for speeding! In Iraq, people drive without driver's licenses and drive the wrong way on one-way streets. Nobody gets tickets for anything — it is a free-for-all.

The almost-empty Illinois land in December was buried beneath 4 inches of snow. I had never seen snow. I wish I could say it was beautiful, but it was not beautiful to me. Iraq is warm year-round and snow is cold. My light shoes would not do in America. I also walked with a crutch and, as I rode to Champaign, I worried that I might slip, fall and hurt myself badly.

"It will look different in the summer," Professor Holley assured me. "Full of corn."

I settled into a room at Professor Holley's house — a house that I thought resembled nothing so much as the homes on Wisteria Lane in "Desperate Housewives," which I watched on satellite TV in Iraq. I had my own bathroom. Everyone in Professor Holley's house had a bathroom of their own! And hot water all the time, not just on the rare day when there is electricity for a couple of hours.

Although the university was on winter break, I went with Professor Holley to her campus office. A student or two dropped in to visit, and I noticed they called her "Lynn." That would never happen in Iraq, but I figured it was normal in America, and I finally had a name to call my hostess.

Many things struck me. For one, the University of Illinois is not like an Iraqi university. Baghdad University is surrounded by a tall wall and protected by armed guards. One circular street takes cars through the campus. The University of Illinois is like a town itself, or maybe it is just all over the town. On campus were churches, flower shops, clothing shops, drugstores, bars, restaurants, even a graveyard.

Champaign-Urbana had restaurants of all flavors — Chinese, Thai, Korean, Italian, Indian, Japanese, Greek, Mexican, even Arabic. In Iraq, we had only Iraqi food: rice, vegetables, tomato sauces, chicken, lamb, beef, fish, cheeses and breads. I love Iraqi food. I came to miss Iraqi food. But all the restaurants meant more than food choices to me. They meant that in America, people were open to the gifts of other nationalities, and they were even willing to pay to try them. I was surprised at the many students from foreign countries and how welcome we were made to feel. American students asked me so many questions about my country. They were interested and sincere, and they wanted to listen, not talk. I had heard many, many stories in Iraq about how Americans hate Arabs and don't want us in their country. When a woman said to me, "I'm sorry for what our president did to your country and we are ashamed of it," I was amazed. America was a far more complicated place than I had known.

Yet most of all I was amazed at the many students with disabilities. I saw students who could barely move either hand and used only their fingers to work their wheelchair controls, students with full-time personal helpers to push their chairs, take their notes, help them to the bathroom. At no cost to the students! I learned of blind students who are given guide dogs so they can go anywhere they wish — the dogs are even allowed in restaurants. I did not know about the university's Disability Resources and Educational Services, known as DRES, before I arrived at Illinois. But DRES sent a bus to pick me up one day so I could visit its offices. A nice lady there told me about how the local bus system and a special university bus accommodate people with disabilities. She showed me the DRES gym. She told me that DRES offers free physical therapy to its clients. I discovered that students with disabilities have special dorms and people to help them get into and out of bed, make meals and do their homework.

"What kind of country is this?" I thought. "What kind of humanity?"

I'm sad to say that this does not exist — and is unlikely ever to exist — in Iraq. I'm sad to say that people in Iraq seem just not to care, or not to care enough about those who are weak. People with so-called flaws are thought never to be able to amount to anything, so we do not try to help them. In Iraq, I was the only student with a disability in any of my schools all the way through college. It was because my parents, both high school teachers, insisted that I be allowed to attend school. At Baghdad University, I struggled up three flights of stairs to attend classes. It took me 15 minutes. Anyone with a worse disability just couldn't go to class. I know that Iraq isn't as rich as America and that such humane services are expensive. Yet I do not believe that is the explanation. In Iraq, even if it were as rich as America, people would simply not think about doing this for people.

I'm sorry, we are a selfish people. Why, I don't know. I just know it is true.

I have been in America a year now, and still my head spins with impressions. College students come to class with coffee and laptop computers. In Iraq, students are not even allowed to chew gum. Students in America argue with professors. That is strange to me. In Iraq, nobody argues with a teacher. If you do, you are likely to get low marks, even fail. No appeal. American students come to class looking as if they have just rolled out of bed, looking like street people. And, I'm sorry, but so many American college kids are brats. They care for their friends more than they care for their parents. They argue with their parents and disrespect them to their faces. They take money and cars and clothes from their parents, and they still whine and complain about not having enough or the best or the most popular. This would never happen in Iraq, and I think that is good. I can't imagine raising children such as those in America. And some things in America were too much like those in Iraq. For instance, the bureaucrats at the U. S. Social Security Agency were about as rude and lazy as the bureaucrats in Iraq, although I did not have to pay a bribe to get my paperwork processed as I would back home.

The famous American malls did not impress me. They were filled with nice things, yes, but so many unnecessary things. People cannot wear so many clothes — Americans must forget what they have in their closets. The malls also are boring. In Iraq, we do not have so many choices, but our marketplaces of small shops, restaurants, coffee shops, hair salons and food stores with live chickens, sheep and fish are teeming with people talking, laughing, mingling, catching up on the gossip. We know the shop owners, and we know the people shopping next to us. Everyone is bartering for better prices. For Americans, I can compare it only to the characters in the American movie "My Big Fat Greek Wedding." The Greek family is like all Iraqi families — loud, pushy, opinionated and always fun, always teasing one another about the dumb things we have done over the years.

Yet so wonderful about America is that everyone is left alone to live their beliefs — Christian, Jew, Muslim, Baha'i, Buddhist, Sikh, atheists, even Satanists. People live and let live. During the U.S. presidential election, Americans hollered, ranted and criticized during the campaign and then, on the night Barack Obama was elected, hundreds of thousands of people of all ages, colors and religions gathered in Chicago's Grant Park to celebrate his victory. His opponent, John McCain, gave a touching, heartfelt speech of congratulations, asking Americans to unite behind Obama. As I watched the evening on TV, I was glad for America, and I was terribly, terribly sad for my country.

Never could that happen in Iraq. Not in a hundred years.

That first day when Professor Holley drove me to Champaign, I worried that I might fall on the ice and hurt myself, and indeed that happened twice in the coming months. The falls put my back in constant and excruciating pain — and led to the greatest miracle that could ever have happened to a young woman from faraway Baghdad. Falaah, my friend in Chicago, insisted that I see a doctor about the pain. I hate doctors. In Iraq, doctors never did anything for me, only looked at the S-shaped X-ray of my spine and told me nothing could be done. But the American doctor, Steven Mardjetko at the Illinois Bone & Joint Institute, was not discouraging.

"We will fix you," he said.

It was a risky surgery with a 20 percent chance that I would end up para-lyzed. But Dr. Mardjetko said I would be in a wheelchair or confined to my bed in five years without the surgery. I trusted him. My friend Falaah pored over my UI graduate student insurance policy and determined that it would cover most of the surgery's cost. I was afraid but I was certain. The two surgeries took Dr. Mardjetko and his team of doctors and nurses a total of 15 hours. I was in the hospital or nursing care for 100 days, and Falaah visted me almost every day. The pain was so bad I cried many times.

"You are going to hate me now," Dr. Mardjetko had told me before the opera-tions, "but after six months you will thank me."

He was right. Six months later, I thank him. The S-curve in my spine is gone. I stand straight now, 4 inches taller than I was. When I saw my body in the mir-ror for the first time after the surgery, I felt as if it was not me, as if this body be-longed to someone else. I was so happy. It was me! I no longer wear bulky clothes to hide my misshapen torso. I wear size 2, petite. I will always walk with a cane, but I will always be able to walk.

I did not tell anyone in Iraq about my surgeries ahead of time. I knew that my father would try to talk me out of the operations. So, after the second surgery and more than a month in the hospital, I text-messaged my parents and told them the doctors said I needed surgery. As expected, my father was in a panic when he called me. I told him to calm down, that I had already gone through the surgeries and that I was fine. He did not believe me until Falaah told him the same thing.

"You are reborn," my mother said.

So it has been quite a year. I was plucked out of Iraq, flown to America, edu-cated and then saved from a life of physical pain and misery. God must have been at work. He made Lynn Holley hear the NPR report. He introduced me to Falaah. He made me fall. He sent me to Dr. Mardjetko. I am not a religious zealot. But I believe God rewards people, and I believe he has rewarded me.

I returned to Champaign and my classes to one more surprise. Professor Harrington had arranged for me to visit the White House and State Department in Washington last fall, so I could see how press operations worked in those in-stitutions. As I walked through the White House's northwest security gate, my mind was racing. I was entering the White House! How many Iraqis will ever visit the White House except for the prime minister? Then, as I sat in the White House press briefing room, President Bush's spokeswoman, Dana Perino, actu-ally welcomed me by name.

"We are also honored to have Zina Bhaia with us today," Ms. Perino said. "Where is she? There she is. Hi. ... So, welcome to you. We're glad you're here."

I nodded a silent thank-you to Dana Perino — and to so many others.

My mother said, "You are reborn." I believe that I am.

Zina Bhaia was born and raised in Baghdad, Iraq, where she received her bachelor's degree in English language from the University of Baghdad. In Baghdad, she worked at various places, including a local radio station called Al-Mahaba. During her work at the station in 2007, she was offered financial support to pursue a master's degree in broadcast journalism from the University of Illinois. She earned her master's degree in fall 2009. Currently, Zina is married and raising two children near Chicago.

Photo by Darrell Hoemann/The News-Gazette

SLICES OF LIFE
36

7

"I'm just grateful"

By Megan Graham

In his old room in his parents' home, a pretty house in the Cherry Hills subdivision of Champaign, Chike Coleman is poking through his shelves. He wants to find a Blu-ray disc, one of the beloved movies he bought in a half-off online sale from a site that sells independent films. He moves aside tens of his prized jazz CDs, the Soapbox Derby trophies and the Hardy Boys books. The shelves are filled with 25 years of memories: books he has loved, model cars done in candy-colored lacquer, his University of Illinois diploma.

His high school and college friends — most 25-year-olds, for that matter — no longer live in the dust of their boyhood belongings. But after his fleeting years of collegiate freedom, Chike moved right back into this room, with its boxes of waterproof dressing and nonstick pads and bandages, bottles of hydrogen peroxide, soap-free cleanser and Clindamycin gel.

"It's just kind of waiting," he says. "Just like everybody else. Except your wait feels a lot shorter than everybody else's."

Chike glances at a photograph of him leaning back casually in his wheelchair, royal blue graduation gown draping his chest as he smiles broadly. He looks normal. He looks healthy.

Yet these are two things Chike will never be.

Chike — pronounced Chee-kay — was born with a rare genetic disorder: chronic granulomatous disease, an immune deficiency that hinders his body from fighting off fungal and bacterial infections. The condition was once called "fatal granulomatosus of childhood." But with medical progress — vaccines, surgical abscess drainage and better medicines — it is no longer necessarily fatal. One victim lived to be 63. Four out of five sufferers, of which there are only about 1,200 in the country, are boys. Many never live to become men.

Life with the chronic granulomatous is difficult, but Chike's cerebral palsy makes it even harder. He cannot walk without a walker. He can suffer from multiple infections at once that come from any of the millions of invasives most people breathe in and fight off. They come without warning, and he often doesn't know he has them until a doctor points them out.

"There's absolutely no way to know," he says. "It could get worse for me. It could get better right now. It's kind of in the worse column, but ..."

When he commented to a blogger with similar health problems, "My body is constantly fighting WWIII," he wasn't exaggerating.

Every day is filled with calculated risks:

Does he balance on the legs of his chair to reach up and get a plate so he can make a meal for himself?

Does he hoist himself up into the newly remodeled bath that is utterly dangerous when slippery?

Does he climb out of his manual wheelchair in his room and down the stairs to his electric chair yet another time that day to get the one small thing he forgot downstairs, knowing full well he could slip and get a cut or bruise that could take forever to heal?

The answer is usually, "Yes."

"I could be a germaphobe and still get hit with something."

Chike has two very different kinds of days: neverending days at home and days out in the dangerous, dirty world. On the dangerous days, he catches the 8:25 a.m. bus. Some days he goes to film his three weekly TV shows at Urbana Public Television, two about film and one about sports. Some days he goes for physical therapy to keep his leg muscles loose.

Being out and about so much may not be wise. The Chronic Granulomatous Association says, "Remember, you cannot be too cautious with your health."

People with Chike's disease are not supposed to work with hay or grass clippings, go barefoot, play at a park with wood chips, go into barns, repot house plants, go inside newly renovated buildings or go near construction sites. People like Chike need to tell the doctor immediately if they have a fever. They are supposed to be vigilant, supposed to live in fear.

"You do end up playing that head game with yourself, worried that you're not doing enough to keep yourself going," he says. "I just can't do that."

As a boy, the wheelchair made Chike feel special, like a pint-sized celebrity. Girls couldn't get enough of the boy with the wheels. In high school, though, he got looks, ones he viewed as saying, "What the hell are you doing invading the space of us normal people?"

The cerebral palsy, though certainly something he has struggled with, he at least understood. He was slower to grasp that he could die at any time. That realization came in pieces. He remembers overhearing his parents talking about it with other adults and slowly understanding that something was terribly wrong with his body. As children his own age grew stronger, he began to realize all the things he couldn't do. He wondered in high school if he'd live to see his graduation day. The fears resurfaced in college, when he began to worry that he could die without saying goodbye to his parents, sister and friends. His deepest fear is that he'll die tonight without time to tell them.

Chike spends much of his time in his bedroom on the Internet, often going downstairs only for meals.

"Even hermits gotta eat!" he says.

He blogs about movies and chats with friends he meets online. The Internet provides a mobility he doesn't have in life. It even allows for a little bit of romance now and then.

"Ninety-five percent of the time I feel like I don't have a chance with any girl."

Online, that can be a different story.

One night, after perusing his OKCupid matches, he started up a conversation with a young woman whose virtual compatibility with his profile was too much to ignore. As they chatted another night, she asked him his real name.

"Chike," he typed.

"How is that pronounced?" she asked. "Does it rhyme with Mike?"

"No it does not. Chee-kay."

And they quickly delved into his conditions.

"Frankly, I'm surprised my disability doesn't frighten you."

"I'm a bit … concerned, I guess," she typed. "But writing someone off completely because of that — well, that's just plain mean."

They chatted through the night, for nearly six hours. She took his phone number and said she would think about text messaging him. He really hoped she would.

Most of his free time, Chike listens to jazz — a favorite recording of Chicago jazz vocalist Kurt Elling and his trio is playing just now. He knows every inflection, scat and purr of this particular recording from 2006. He sings in his room, his left hand — his good hand — gripping the computer mouse, his right hand in its permanent position with thumb and finger forming an askew U, the three remaining fingers curled into his palm. As he sways his small frame in his chair, the pointer finger of his right hand hits the tempo up and down as if he is conducting.

He does the Louis Armstrong voice, deep and scratchy and round, with his eyes squeezed shut, his head bowed and a smile on his face. He does the Nat King Cole voice, smooth and silken and weightless, leaning back and tilting his face skyward. He pretends to smoke a cigarette, something he would never do in real life. His health is bad enough.

Every night before sleep, Chike allows himself five minutes for tears. "Five minutes a night," he says. "That's all I get."

It's never because of any particular difficult moment of his day or because of his terrible genetic luck. It's because of the collection of millions of hardships and fears and uncertainties he feels at every moment, the awareness that at any second, during sleep or waking hours, some Aspergillus fumigatus or Blastomyces dermatitidis or Cryptococcus could creep into his body.

He wonders: Will I die in my sleep from something the doctors haven't found? Or will medicine progress so that I might live long and healthy?

"I just keep going the best I can."

The past few weeks have brought hope to Chike. The girl from OKCupid finally texted him back. She wrote, "Boo." They've been chatting every day since, and he can't stop smiling. He also was accepted into the journalism graduate program at the University of Illinois. He's expecting at least one new friend, some difficult classes and the rekindled independence of apartment life back on campus.

Of course, the apartment search isn't going smoothly — nothing ever does. In the first one he toured, his wheelchair got stuck on a rainbow knotted rug and the chair wouldn't fit in the bathroom. The second wasn't much better.

"You know, I'm going into it with some trepidation," he says. "Am I going to get through this without an incident?"

Yet Chike's determined to stay optimistic, hoping graduate school will lead to a life beyond the walls of his boyhood room and the confines of his disease.

After all of it, he says simply, "I'm just grateful."

Megan Graham, from Downers Grove, Ill., is a business and features journalist in Chicago. A former business reporter for the Kokomo (Ind.) Tribune, she is currently a staff reporter for the Chicago Sun-Times' business magazine, Grid. In 2012, she traveled to Turkey as part of a Social Science Research Council-sponsored trip to report on Syrian refugees in the border region. Her coverage of Turkish cuisine was published in the International Herald Tribune. Megan is a 2012 news-editorial journalism graduate from the University of Illinois.

8

Wonderful waltz

By Richard Anderson

Frances and Mitch Harris treasure these five minutes. They have plodded through the evening, trading partners and sharing laughs, surrendering to the spirit of community dance. Now they get to dance alone, together.

Frances and Mitch follow this routine every other Friday at the contra dances they have attended together for 11 years. This is where and how they met — at a contra dance in the Phillips Recreation Center in Urbana — same building, same room. He was a bachelor. She was divorced. A decade later, they are married — and still in love.

"I always really liked dancing with him," Frances says. "And I still do."

Frances and Mitch are happy. Their home is clean and comfortable, hand-some and dignified. They go to temple and volunteer around town. They have made it as a married couple. Frances and Mitch are older and busier than when they started dancing together. On Friday nights now they are tired and usually leave the dance early. But that's OK. Contra dance will always be the melody that keeps the time of their romance.

"I kind of like the randomness of it, how it all works," Frances says of contra dancing. "All of a sudden you're in somebody else's arms and it's like magic."

During the first half of the 20th century contra dance thrived mainly in New England. Since the 1960s, it has spread across the United States to big cities and smaller communities like Urbana. Contra is similar to square dance in its use of intricate patterns directed by a caller. Contra dance evolved from "longways" English country dance, in which male and female partners form long lines oppo-site one another. Couples execute a series of simple moves — spins, promenades, do-si-dos — with each other and with the couple next to them. Then both couples shift in opposite directions on the line and repeat the same moves with another couple.

Contra dances are always accompanied by live music, and tonight's band

Photo by Heather Coit/The News-Gazette

SLICES OF LIFE
42

has come from Chicago with guitars, mandolins and fiddles. Most contra dances involve long sets, around 10 minutes, that gradually increase in pace. But the last dance before intermission is always a waltz.

And Frances and Mitch waltz only with each other. The fiddles take up a slow, melancholy tune. They loop around again and again in three-quarter time, guiding the dancers with the beat. Normally, the caller directs the dancers' movements. But nobody needs a caller for a waltz. The dancers can feel it — just step and slide and one-two-three, one-two-three. The fiddlers drop their instruments to their laps and harmonize:

> *There's more pretty girls than one*
> *more pretty girls than one*
> *every town I rambled around*
> *there's more pretty girls than one.*

The lyrics make for an unlikely accompaniment because for this couple there is no more wandering. For Mitch there is only Frances, and for Frances there is only Mitch.

Tonight is "Hawaiian Shirt Night" (wear one and admission is half-price). Mitch sports an untucked purple shirt with a white floral pattern. He always wears jeans when he dances.

He is 46 with a bald spot beginning to creep outward from the crown of his head. His face is boyish and round. He keeps his graying beard thick. Mitch wears eyeglasses on a face that always remains serene on the dance floor. He's been contra dancing for more than 20 years.

Frances has been contra dancing since the night she met Mitch. She is 55. She wears glasses, too. Her face is all rosy cheekbones. It's a young face with few lines. It's a face that giggles and grins. Frances keeps her dark hair in short layers around her face and neck. Tonight she wears a black blouse, black skirt with white checks, and black tights. She and Mitch both wear sneakers with customized rubber soles for dancing. He is taller by a couple of inches, and she tilts her head upward to meet his glance.

Frances and Mitch are feeling the dance. They step and slide — one-two-three, one-two-three. On step three, they pivot and change direction. A dozen other couples zigzag around them with varying degrees of accuracy as the band continues its ballad:

> *Mama talked to me last night*
> *She gave me some good advice*
> *She said, "Son, you'd better quit*

this old ramblin' all around
and marry you a sweet little wife."

Frances and Mitch met in fall 1997. The last three years had been difficult for Frances. She and her husband of 19 years had divorced in 1994. Frances worked as the librarian at University Laboratory High School in Urbana and raised her sons, Simon and Daniel.

"I remember just real insecurity about pretty basic things," she recalls. "Like how much would groceries cost, or actually, more basic than that, just the trip to the grocery store, getting everything loaded into the car, brought in and put away. I mean a lot of those things that used to be done together."

The loneliness was crushing, especially on nights when the boys would stay with their father.

"That was pretty awful because the house was cavernous and empty and weird," Frances says.

Yet she shuttled the boys to school and music lessons, paid the bills and took care of the house. She didn't date for a few years but then began thinking about companionship again.

"It was definitely in the back of my mind that this might happen, but it was also just about getting out and seeing people," she says. Her sons didn't make up for the lack of affection. "They were not cuddling anymore."

Then a friend invited her to a contra dance where she met Mitch, who was not at all familiar with Frances' world of family and kids.

"You were raising kids," he says as he and Frances sit close on their living room couch. "I was raising my IRA."

Mitch grew up in Newton, Mass., and studied biology at Grinnell College in Iowa, where he started contra dancing.

"I remember when I first 'got' waltzing. I was dancing with this tall African-American woman at Grinnell, maybe 6 feet tall, and she just swung me around until I thought, 'Hey, I can do this.'"

After college, Mitch entered his "wandering days." He had biology-related jobs in South Carolina, California, Oregon and Colorado, where he earned a master's degree at Colorado State University. Mitch contra danced everywhere he went. He moved to Urbana in 1991 to work for the Illinois Natural History Survey (he now works for the U.S. Geological Survey) and began looking for a contra dance group.

"That was probably the first thing I did."

Mitch and his new contra dance friends would dance for hours every Friday night and then go for beers. Contra dancing gave Mitch his social life and his dating life. He grins and shifts in his seat when asked how many contra dancers he dated.

"Let's just say 'a few,'" he says. By the time Mitch met Frances, he was in his mid-30s and had never married.

"I guess I was still young, but it was getting toward the time it would be nice to meet someone," Mitch says. "I kind of just waited for things to happen. But they never quite happened. I probably made a mistake by leaving the East Coast where all the Jewish girls were."

Then he saw Frances and asked her to dance. She mentioned her sons and was relieved that Mitch seemed unfazed. Later at the dance, he strategically mentioned that he would not attend the following week because of the Jewish high holidays. Frances, who was raised Jewish, was not observant at the time and joked back, "My mother probably wishes I was staying home for the high holidays."

Mitch is a member of B'nai B'rith, the national Jewish fraternal organization, and Frances knew her mother would be happy.

"When I got married I was still rebelling. I was a child of the '60s. My own Jewish upbringing was pretty hit-and-miss. And I had a lot of resentment about it. So, I was actively rejecting it."

A few weeks after meeting Mitch at the dance, Frances and her sons returned home to find the red light on the answering machine blinking. The three of them listened together. It was a message from Mitch, asking her out for the first time.

"You are too old to date!" 13-year-old Simon exclaimed. "And button your shirt all the way up!"

On their first date, Mitch brought Frances chrysanthemums from his yard. They went to see Chinese dancers at the Krannert Center for the Performing Arts.

"OK, I just have to know," Frances asked Mitch, "how old are you?"

The nine-year difference didn't scare him off. Frances also wasn't scared off at intermission when they bumped into one of Mitch's former girlfriends, a contra dancer. They survived the moment, and Frances became Mitch's new contra-dance girlfriend.

The waltz continues, and Mitch moves with controlled grace. He is not fancy and he wastes no movements. Some dancers dip and skip. He remains upright and his face remains tranquil. Frances dances with a perpetual grin. She approaches dancing differently than Mitch. He counts and visualizes the patterns. Frances feels the rhythm and takes her cues from the music.

"When I started talking to people at the dances," Frances says, "it seemed there were more than your usual number of programmers or science types. And I'm not that way at all. For me it's much more intuitive."

"Yeah," Mitch says, laughing, "I'm part of the science crowd."

Somewhere between Mitch's left brain and Frances' right, things worked out.

"It was just really comfortable right away," Frances remembers. "We were cut from the same cloth."

Mitch doesn't remember when he knew that Frances was "the one." Things just flowed. Frances remembers him sitting on the floor with Simon, helping her son with his math homework.

Two years after their first dance, Frances and Mitch were engaged.

In May 2000 they were married.

Frances and Mitch still love to waltz with each other, and only each other.

They have slid to the corner of the hall, next to the stage. The band brings the melody around once more to the chorus:

There's more pretty girls than one
more pretty girls than one
every town I rambled around
there's more pretty girls than one.

Mitch and Frances are all smiles. They step and slide — one-two- three, one-two-three. The fiddle signals the last note. Frances and Mitch move a last beat or two and glide to a halt. They are still clasping hands. He leans over and kisses her cheek. The dance is done. Frances and Mitch go home, together.

Richard Anderson grew up in Pittsfield, Mass. He completed his bachelor's degree in history from Northeastern Illinois University in 2006 and received a master's degree in journalism at the University of Illinois in 2008. At Illinois, he covered grassroots political activism and suburban development southwest of Chicago. Richard combined his dedication to historical scholarship, interviewing and civic engagement by pursuing a master's degree in public history from the University of Massachusetts, which he completed in 2011. He is currently a doctoral candidate in American history at Princeton University, where he coordinates the history department's Public History Initiative. Richard contributes to the National Council for Public History's blog site, History@Work.

9

A sacred fire

By Claire (Benjamin) Sturgeon

I'm a farmer's daughter, but I can't navigate the grain elevator, grease the combine or repair fence lines. I have never mucked a hog pen or delivered a stillborn lamb. My children will not build hay forts on my family farm or dams in the creek down the road. They will not tame herds of kittens or rescue baby birds from fallen nests. No more rotten apple wars. No more evenings of catching lightning bugs to feed to pet toads — their bellies flickering.

I'm the end of the line, the end of an era. After my dad retires, our land will be rented out until it is gobbled up by Bloomington's urban sprawl.

Thomas Jefferson once said, "Those who labour in the earth are the chosen people of God, if ever he had a chosen people, whose breasts he has made his peculiar deposit for substantial and genuine virtue. It is the focus in which he keeps alive that sacred fire, which otherwise might escape from the face of the earth."

It hurts that this flame has been snuffed out in me, that I cannot count myself as one of these chosen people. As a senior at the University of Illinois, I've picked a different life. A life in an office, working — I hope — as a journalist. A life far removed from back-breaking work days, devastating droughts and broken machinery. A life with a husband who is concerned about Internet connectivity rather than grain futures.

Yet I always enjoy returning to the family farm for harvest. Each year, I come home to ride a few rounds with my dad in the combine. My excitement at being again among fields the color of spun-honey grows as I drive away from Champaign-Urbana and my pile of chapters that should be read. Eventually, I spot the neon Love's sign off Interstate 74 in LeRoy, a signal I'm almost home. The sun dances along the bean stubble, and I think of the Grinch's small heart growing three sizes and imagine that mine must be growing as well.

I turn down 1300 N toward Bentown — a town that was founded in 1853 under its former name, Benjaminville, after my great-great-great-grandfather John R. Benjamin. Today it's almost a ghost town. All that remains are a few houses

Photo provided by Benjamin family

and an abandoned Friends Meeting House.

I pass by the O'Neall farmstead. I don't recognize the car in Rusty Benjamin's drive. I try to spot members of Carmen's animal menagerie as I pass her patchwork of pens. I drive by my mom's house, a quarter mile east of my dad's farm, but I can't tell if she's home. Before they divorced six years ago, she helped my dad farm full time for 13 years, cultivating ground in the spring and hauling grain in the fall. That's how I know I could do it, too. If only there was enough land to take over. If only our machinery wasn't old. If only I wanted to.

"Hi, dad, I'm home!" I trill when I walk into the kitchen. My dad walks out of his office holding a small stack of papers and running his fingers through his thick, salt-and-pepper hair. His wide, sunburned face breaks into a smile.

"We have to get gas for the truck this morning," he says.

"That's fine," I reply as I mix a glass of Ovaltine.

"This bid is below the other local elevator's, so I'm going to confront him about it," he says of an elevator manager to whom he usually sells a portion of his corn and beans.

"Hi, this is George Benjamin," my dad says into the phone. "I wanted to confirm we got the percentages correct. I was looking at your bid online and wondered why your bid was 7 cents less. LeRoy is 15.93." He pauses to listen. "I'm going to sell the beans then at 15.93. And Mildred Benjamin-Smiddy, I'm going to sell hers the same way. Thank you."

He hangs up.

"I'm very tickled with that," he says, smiling, as we pull on our work boots.

It bothers me that my Redwings look shiny and new beside his pair with their scratched, worn leather. But that's part of the life I've chosen. We make a quick run to Bloomington to fill up the truck and get to work preparing the machinery for the day at the original Benjamin farmstead, a quarter-mile down the road, where we store our machinery and my brother's European fallow deer herd.

I watch as my dad tries to connect a shaft onto the feeder house on the bean head. He shoves the part into position with his thigh and bangs on it with a hammer. After a few more minutes of shoving, readjusting and hammering, the piece finally falls into place.

Hours later, the beans have finally dried out enough to begin harvest. I barely adjust myself in the combine's buddy seat beside my dad when my brother Neal calls to see if I can help him tranquilize and move one of his deer to a neighbor's land. He is a first-year UI student in veterinary medicine, his chosen career ever since I can remember.

Neal picks me up at the southwest field entrance, and a minute later we pull up at the farm, studied by five pairs of black eyes. For 9 years, Rocky had been his herd's stag, but a younger buck has begun to challenge his dominance due to Rocky's age and his tumorous growth. The deer are skittish. They prance in circles around Neal as he pivots in the center of the 7-foot pen. The dart hits Rocky low on his left hind leg.

"Adrenaline can override the drugs, so you don't want to excite him," Neal cautions as I enter the pen. I have never really been in the deer pen before. As a child, I was warned that the deer can be dangerous, even deadly. But on his belly, legs folded beneath him, Rocky is purring like a cat. He struggles to stand, and his head sways back and forth like a drunkard.

"I don't think he is going to go all the way under," Neal says. "We will have to walk him out."

He latches onto Rocky's antlers and pulls. Rocky strains against him, his knees lock and his legs bow. But with the tranquilizer, Rocky is not strong enough to resist. The drug appears to be wearing off by the time we arrive at our neighbor's house where Rocky will stay. I cringe as his body slams into the side of the truck on the way to his pen. After Neal guides him through the gate, Rocky backs away and lies down, again succumbing to the drugs.

On the drive home, my pulse slows, and I feel proud. I had helped manhandle a full-grown buck. I felt a match strike somewhere deep inside me. That sacred fire Thomas Jefferson says burns in those who toil in the earth had been re-kindled inside me.

But I know the truth: On the farm, I am out of place, a book housed in the wrong genre. Neal drops me back at the southwest field entrance, and I climb up into the combine cab beside my dad.

As we ease into yet another conversation about bean production, a high beeping sound fills the cab telling us the combine has broken down.

It has just gotten dark when I return more than an hour later after "gophering" parts from Clinton to repair the combine. My dad and our hired man, Curt Harrison, are clanging on the combine. My dad hands me a flashlight and picks up a long crowbar.

With all his weight, he pulls against the lock collar holding the broken bearing onto the combine shaft. Curt pulls on the crowbar that is under the opposite edge of the lock collar. They grimace with effort.

After a minute or two, they switch approaches. Curt places a hole punch in a screw hole on the lock collar and hits it with a 2-pound hammer. The lock collar slowly revolves around the bearing with each hit. But it doesn't budge. Soon my dad breaks out a blow torch. A blue flame heats the metal. An hour later, after countless attempts using the torch, punch and crowbars, the lock collar loosens and they wrench it off.

I'm proud of my dad's tenacity, his calm and persistent demeanor. He hardly pauses even to celebrate before turning his attention to the bearing. We spend another unproductive hour trying to loosen the bearing without success. Finally, without a hint of discouragement, my dad announces that we should call it night.

On the drive home, I feel helpless and frustrated. I hate giving up. I hate not knowing if we would break that bearing if we worked on it for five more minutes or five more days. I hate knowing that I couldn't have wrangled Rocky or broken that lock collar myself. I hate being at Mother Nature's mercy. I hate knowing that this year, with the drought, our yields won't add up to my dad's long hours and strenuous work.

"I would just like to say I'm tired," my dad says when we walk through the front door. We kick off our boots, and I am pleased to see my Redwings looking a little less new.

Later that evening, my dad and I talk about the farm. We talk about how it was when he was a kid. We talk about how he wouldn't want me to take over the farm because no one knows when the good years will run out. We talk about how he's the last of six generations to farm the original Benjaminville land.

I try not to cry, but a few tears slide down my cheeks. I forget about the broken bearing and drought-devastated yields. I can only picture the sun-dappled fields and that feeling of sitting in the humming combine surrounded by illuminated dust and a love for the land and the season and my dad. Pride for our farm, the generations before me and this little place called Bentown burns inside me.

Even if I cannot stay, it will stay within me.

Claire (Benjamin) Sturgeon was born to a farm family from Ellsworth, Ill. She was the fifth generation from her family to attend the University of Illinois and study agriculture. In 2013, she earned a bachelor's degree in agricultural communications with a minor in crop and soil management. Her news-editorial concentration and drive to tell untold stories of rural life led her to take Walt Harrington's journalism course. Claire was a communications intern for the College of Agricultural, Consumer and Environmental Sciences. She also worked as a youth ambassador for the Illinois Farm Bureau and as a social-media intern for the Illinois Corn Growers Association. Today, she is a media communications specialist for the Institute for Genomic Biology at the University of Illinois. This story won first place in both the long-feature-story category and the overall writing category in the National Agricultural Communicators of Tomorrow's award program.

Photo by Darrell Hoemann/The News-Gazette

SLICES OF LIFE

10

Jessie's first fight

By Thomas Bruch

One ...

Jessie Bushman's back grazes the top rope of the ring, making it vibrate gently in contrast to the violence all around. Her hands, mummy-wrapped and fitted with two red gloves, are pinned to her abdomen. She's trying to breathe.

Two ...

Jessie is in a cavernous shed next to Ruth Lake Country Club west of Chicago — her first round in her first fight as an amateur boxer. Tall lights shine in four corners of the shed lighting the ring, elevated just above the ground-level chairs. Her opponent has been ordered to the opposite side of the ring by a referee with a crew cut and thick mustache. Jessie's inhales and exhales are short, terse.

Not enough.

Three ...

She's getting a standing eight-count from the referee after four consecutive blows to the head. The first punch, a right hook that connected on her left chin, knocked Jessie off her footing. She staggered slightly, her right foot awkwardly crossing her left. Her arms dropped and her body became a vulnerable offering. Jessie extended her arms, but her opponent plunged through the halfhearted defense and mashed Jessie's head three more times with two hooks and a loop.

The referee stepped between the fighters to halt the mayhem. Jessie doesn't register any repercussive effects of the punches. But her lungs, they plead for air.

Four ...

Before the fight, 25-year-old Jessie was too excited to be nervous. She had trained for eight months at Luyando's, the little boxing gym tucked near downtown Champaign, molding a body she once considered physically adequate into what she thought was a jabbing, 141-pound wrecking ball.

The boxing had started as exercise classes for Jessie and her girlfriends. She had rarely played sports growing up, just a few years of volleyball in middle school. But she liked staying in shape. She and her friends giggled while waiting their turn at a punching bag, fearing that the gym's real boxers would cut them in line. Slowly, Jessie's friends stopped coming. Jessie remained.

For reasons she really can't explain, she decided she wanted to get strong and good enough to fight an actual match. Jessie is a gentle soul, shy and soft-spoken. Crystal blue eyes, clear skin, long brown hair, 5 foot 8.

She owns Bella Vita Massage in Champaign, and her body has always been well-muscled for a woman. But she wasn't carrying a deep anger that made her want to punch somebody or harboring a fearfulness that made her want to learn to defend herself physically. She just wanted to get in the ring once and fight.

Thirty minutes before tonight's match, Jessie suited up in the changing room, adjusting her protective bra shells, tightening the blue shorts that drape to her knees, yanking her mahogany hair back into a tight ponytail. Nelson Luyando, her stocky coach who grew up boxing in the Bronx, shadowboxed with her to warm up.

Once in the shed, she scanned the room for her opponent, not a difficult task considering she was the only other boxer in the place with breasts. They locked eyes for a moment. She seemed normal.

Oddly, Jessie wondered what the young woman's body-fat percentage was.

Five ...

When music and cheers mushroomed, Jessie walked toward the illuminated ring. She couldn't remember a time when a crowd was watching only her. Maybe those volleyball games in middle school, but far different.

She saw a crowd of about 100 men who were spiritedly sauced for a night at the fights. They were betting on the many scheduled matches, and some had their money on Jessie.

She paced in her corner, then shifted her weight from one leg to the other, then jogged in place. In the seconds before the match began, she wondered if she and her opponent would touch gloves after the bell had rung? And would she remember to retreat to a neutral corner if her opponent's mouth guard fell out?

Getting her head bashed repeatedly was not on her mind. Neither were concussions or bruises or drunken men, or even something so simple as breathing.

Six ...

The bell rang. The women touched gloves. It was Jessie's first fight, and she knew her skills were limited, that she had mastered only a few punching combinations. So she focused on keeping her right hand up, at the ready, for defense or for offense. For the first 30 seconds, she was winning, landing jabs and deflecting her opponent's punches. The dance was in motion, and Jessie was leading.

Boxing rounds are only two minutes long, but they're equivalent to a 400-meter sprint. And after a minute, Jessie had lost her breath. She couldn't get enough to fuel her next punch. Her mechanics deteriorated with each halting inhale, and her right hand dropped. Her opponent capitalized, landing those four punches. Each blow felt heavy on impact, more crushing than those of her male sparring partners at Luyando's. But it wasn't the punches. It was the breathing.

Seven ...
Jessie hasn't caught her breath yet, but she wants to keep fighting. Once the referee says eight, she knows he will determine if she can continue.

Eight ...
The referee clutches the sides of Jessie's face and looks into her blinking eyes.

"Can you go?" he asks.

Jessie nods. The referee is convinced. He drops his arm to signal that the fight can resume. Jessie takes two steps forward and the bell rings — Round 1 is over. After 30 seconds in her corner, Nelson motions to Jessie that it's time for the second round.

At least Jessie figures he must have motioned, because she later can't recall a word he had said in those 30 seconds. But here she is, on her feet stepping again toward the middle of the ring. She isn't afraid. She knows she is being beaten. She was confident just two minutes ago, and she tells herself she needs to get back to that feeling. She stares at the woman who had just used Jessie's head as a punching bag. Jessie wants to hit her, hit her back, hit her harder. That's what those punches to the head had caused: a desire for retaliation. Jessie is woozy, but she still plans to get the knockout. That sounds vicious, but her opponent knows what she signed up for. Jessie knows what she signed up for. She's ready.

Except for the breathing.

The referee flings down his arm to start the second round. The women both swing, each landing their first punches. Jessie hangs tough for the first 10 seconds and deflects a few jabs while connecting on some of her own. But the gasping for air comes again, and Jessie is soon lunging and flailing.

Ten seconds and ten shots to Jessie's head later, the referee performs the eight-count on Jessie again, although she's not even noticing the counting.

One ... three ... six ... eight ...

This time, the referee finds nothing in Jessie's crystal blue eyes to indicate she can continue to fight, and he waves his hands to confirm a technical knockout. Jessie absently walks back to her corner, feeling as if the woman had opened her skull and taken a blender to its contents. She sees Nelson and bashfully apologizes.

"What are you talking about? That was great!" an enthused Nelson yells.

She doesn't understand what he means. A few more people, boxers and spectators alike, congratulate her, and after a while Jessie feels like hopping back in the ring and going a few more rounds. She didn't lose any love from anyone by losing the fight. No one thinks less of her. Why would they? It took guts and grit to climb in that ring.

She'll get back to work in the gym. She'll get better. She'll learn more combinations. And she'll work on better breathing techniques, run more wind sprints, pound the bag longer and harder. She will own that ring someday.

And that's pretty much what will happen. In the next three months, a better-trained, better-honed Jessie Bushman will win two fights. New women training at Luyando's will look at her with awe and seek her advice.

"How did you get so good?" they will ask.

And Jessie will have a new goal: To win in the Chicago Golden Gloves amateur competition in March.

Her next fight can't come soon enough.

Thomas Bruch lived in the Peoria, Ill., area for 13 years before attending the University of Illinois. He graduated with a bachelor's degree in news-editorial journalism in 2013. Thomas spent three months interning as a metro/news reporter for the Peoria Journal Star in summer 2012 and returned to the position in summer 2013. Along with reporting, reliving 1990s-era NBA basketball consumes most of his life.

11

"Thanks be to God"

By Allison Copenbarger Vance

As Sarah Roy walks down Sixth Street, her pale blue eyes squint slightly at the sun and her black veil gently whips behind her head. She's among a sea of North Face jackets, Ugg boots and orange and blue sweatpants. She is in her normal garb: black jumper, black tights, black veil and black mary-jane flats. It's the same uniform she has worn nearly every day for the nine years since she became a Roman Catholic nun. Today, she has added a navy hooded sweatshirt over her jumper — it's a little chilly.

The University of Illinois campus is always busy just before noon as students hurry to class. Sarah is instead hurrying to noon Mass at St. John's Catholic Chapel at Sixth and Armory streets. She hops up the familiar concrete steps to the chapel and opens the heavy glass door, above which is carved: "Teach ye all nations all things whatsoever I have commanded you."

Sister Sarah sees the engraving as an assuring reminder: At 33, she is carrying out what God has commanded of her by being a Catholic sister; she is being obedient and useful to God. She is confident in being the only sister younger than 50 in her entire diocese. She wears the habit with pride. She is content with a life of no sex, no husband, no children and no luxuries. But she wasn't always so sure this was where God wanted her or where she wanted to be. And sometimes she still doesn't feel like what she calls a "typical nun."

St. John's sanctuary is massive, with a high, curved, gothic ceiling and giant stained-glass windows. Above the altar is a painting of Jesus and his disciples. It is a Catholic church not unlike the one Sarah grew up with in New Haven, Ind. As she did as a girl, she makes the sign of the cross, kneels, folds her hands and bows her head.

Brrrrriiiiinggggg.

The familiar bell rings. Mass begins.

It was in this sanctuary that Sarah wrestled through the decision to become

Photo by Darrell Hoemann/The News-Gazette

SLICES OF LIFE

a nun. One day about 10 years ago, while she was studying social work in graduate school at the UI, she came here for answers. She needed to know what direction God had for her life.

She began to pray: *God, please don't make me a sister. Just let me find my husband and we'll get married and we'll have 10 children and raise them all Catholic.
Just please, please don't make me a nun.*

After dating Joe, also a devout Catholic, for two years, she still didn't think
he was the one. He was great. They had talked about marriage. But after praying
together about it incessantly she told him their marriage didn't feel right. At first,
she thought maybe Joe just wasn't the one; maybe she would marry someone
else. In St. John's sanctuary, in quiet time with her God, she believed He would
give her the answer she so desperately needed: *God just give me a sign, please just
give me a sign of what you want me to do. Just tell me what you want, please.*

Sarah liked to pray for signs. Although a relationship with God is an intan-
gible thing, throughout her life she believes He has manifested Himself to her in
visible ways.

To her left was a stained-glass window. It read, "And all that heard Him were
astonished at His wisdom and His answers." Sarah heard a sound behind her,
lifted her head and turned to see what the noise could be — she had picked this
time of day because the chapel was usually empty. She saw a nun walking down
the aisle. She was dressed from head to feet in a veil and a long, black skirt. She
seemed to glide down the aisle toward Sarah. She knelt on one knee, stood and
shuffled into the row in front of Sarah.

Ha, ha, that's funny, God. You're so funny. I'm not doing that.

In a mix of fury and fear, Sarah quickly got up and left the chapel.

Brrrrriiiiinggggg.

Sarah lifts her head, listens to a woman in her 20s wearing a gray sweater
and an orange scarf give the first reading. "The word of the Lord," the woman
says.

"Thanks be to God," Sarah responds aloud along with the rest of the
congregation.

Mass was always a familiar experience to Sarah. She attended Catholic
church her whole life. Her parents were Catholic, and she had attended private,
Catholic schools for preschool, middle school and high school. She had attended
church every Sunday since she could remember.

She believes she had her first experience with God in preschool. Sarah's
teacher always read the children Bible stories before naptime. One day, her
teacher told them the story of Samuel from the Old Testament — about how God

called his name, and he didn't listen. Sarah recalls that she was determined not to be like Samuel. She convinced herself in that moment, lying on her back looking up at the ceiling, that when God called her name, she would hear it and get it right the first time.

"I remember I was looking out the window waiting," Sarah says. "It was the first time, in the way a 3-year-old can, that I longed for a relationship with God."

About 20 years later, Sarah thought again about Samuel. God's call for her to a life as a Catholic sister wasn't a clarion call. She didn't hear a deep, rumbling audible voice from the heavens calling down to her as Samuel must have.

Instead, after she had fled from the chapel, God spoke to her through a pros and cons list. She was nearing the end of graduate school for social work. She was praying about her future and decided to take the practical step of listing all the good and bad points of being married versus being a nun.

"I really thought it would weigh toward marriage, and I was trying to make it lean that way," Sarah says. "But in the end it was very clear that I was called to religious life."

After this realization, Sarah pleaded with God: *No, I can't do this, God. I'm quite the sinner! I'm not living the good Christian life in lots of ways. I can't do this.* Later that day, she opened a book she had been reading to this line: "God's arms are the elevator which lifts us up." In that moment, Sarah said she felt like God was saying, "Don't worry, I am going to do it for you."

"It was the weirdest thing," Sarah says with a faraway look in her eyes. "I had been so mad and then, all of the sudden, I was like, 'Well, if you're going to do it for me, then I'll say yes.'"

She has never doubted the decision since.

Brrrrriiiiinggggg.

The robed priest gives a reading from the Bible and then says, "Let us pray."

Sarah bows her head, and her black veil falls closer to her face in prayer.

The decision to wear the veil — or habit — was a difficult one for Sarah. Of the many sisters in her diocese, only about a quarter wear them. After Vatican II, a time in the 1960s when the Roman Catholic Church made reforms, nuns could choose whether or not they would wear a habit or regular clothes. A wave of relief rolled through the sisterhood; they could finally look like everyone else. In her first three years as a nun, Sarah didn't wear a habit and was uncertain if she ever would.

After all, she loved clothes and shopping. When she was growing up, her mother, Laura, bought her a new wardrobe every season. Beginning in high school, Sarah started to highlight her hair every few months. She always kept her toenails polished in bright colors. Yet nuns don't shop and primp. Becoming a sister meant giving that up — along with her car, cell phone, career and income. Finally, she decided to wear the habit.

"I thought, 'Well, I can either look like a sister or a frumpy 30-year-old,'" she says, laughing.

More seriously, Sarah likes that the uniform makes her stand out. She hopes that it makes her look approachable and that it makes people think about God, if even in a small way. It also makes her quite the spectacle. Once, while Sarah was grocery shopping, a man yelled, "Hey, look, it's a nun!" Everyone turned to stare, leaving her mortified. Another time, while in a cashier's line close to Halloween, the students behind her and in front of her thought she was wearing a nun costume. When they found out she was an actual nun, she says they mocked her for not having sex.

"To people, you're not really a person," Sarah explains. "You're this religious freak — a foreign entity."

Her wardrobe consists of four veils and several black jumpers that her stepmom, Karen, made for her to save on cost. She has two pairs of shoes, her black everyday flats and her running shoes. She also has T-shirts, jeans and sweatpants — for relaxing at home or for when she just needs a break and wants to be treated like everybody else at the grocery store. She is also allowed to wear any kind of colored, modest blouse. She said other sisters go to Goodwill or the Salvation Army to save on cost, but she has never done that.

"I guess I'm too vain!" she says.

In accordance with the vow of poverty, she is given $40 a month by St. John's for clothes and spending money. Her mother often buys her running shoes, which are very expensive for someone living on $40 a month.

Not all of her family members understood her desire to become a nun or the spirit of her life. She received so many gift cards after her final vows that the church made a rule that sisters had to turn in all monetary gifts. Her mom invited her out to celebrate her final vows and took her and a few fellow nuns from the convent to a spa day.

"It was OK because it was for the sake of my mom," Sarah says. "Now, if I came down to the chapel with my fingernails painted they'd be like, 'Go upstairs and take that stuff off.' I wouldn't get in trouble, but I'd feel so out of place."

Although Sarah never doubts her call to be a nun, she has doubted being a nun working at the Catholic Newman Center on the University of Illinois campus, where the next-youngest sister is nearly 20 years older than she. She lives with one other sister at the convent across from St. John's, and the rest of the sisters in the diocese live more than 90 miles away in Peoria. The average age of nuns in the diocese is 68.

"I wish there were more younger sisters," she says. "It would be fun instead of trying to relate with people twice my age."

Sarah is cordial but not close with her fellow sisters. Unlike some of the others, she enjoys working out, jogging, tae bo and yoga. She watches "The Biggest Loser." She ran the Champaign Marathon last year. She has a Facebook page; her profile picture shows her with a white, fuzzy snowman cap atop her head.

Her parents often worry about what will happen to Sarah in 30 years. If more younger sisters don't join her community, she could be left to care for everyone else with no one to care for her. Currently she is a spiritual adviser to individual college students and plans group activities such as retreats. Just added to her job was the task of recruiting new sisters. Sarah doesn't worry. She believes God will keep His word and be with her the whole way.

The priest concludes his homily, the congregation stands and says in unison, "Lord, hear our prayer."

Sarah closes her eyes. A little boy with white-blonde hair a few rows ahead is smiling with full, rosy cheeks and bright eyes. Suddenly he trips and falls and cries out. He runs to his mother, who smiles and scoops him up into her arms.

At the noise, Sarah opens her eyes and gazes at the boy and the mom's pregnant belly. She then lowers her head to rest on her steepled hands.

Brrrrriiiiinggggg.

Accepting that she would not have children was a hurdle for Sarah, who had always expected to be a mommy.

But that wasn't God's plan.

Sarah says many sisters go through a grieving process with God about not having children. This hasn't happened to her yet. But she says not having a husband and children is difficult at times. Sometimes she just wants someone to hold her. Last year, when her uncle died, she had no one to console her at the funeral. Her mother had her husband. Her father had his wife. Her brother had his wife. Her other brother had his girlfriend. If the funeral had been closer, Sarah's sisters in community would have come. But it was too far, and she was left alone.

For Sarah, the issue of not having a certain someone is more an issue of emotions than lust. She says celibacy isn't much of a problem for her. What she craves is human intimacy. She looks to God to fill that void.

Since middle school, she has kept a faith journal, writing in it every few days. It helps her focus on God and makes talking to him more real. She also experiences Him through prayer — at least two hours every day. Sister Sarah starts with God at 8 a.m: *God, help me to be more patient with students. God, be with me as I plan the student's retreat today. Help me to feel you today. Help me to love people well.*

"When you get quiet — to a point of just being — and you just sit there listening," she says, "you become very aware of God's presence."

During her prayer time, she believes God has spoken to her through Scripture that solved some problem she was having that day. Sometimes when she has a persistent thought in her head that is unexplainable she believes it is God who has placed the thought in her head. Still, sometimes she longs just to be held — to be shown affection. Sarah says the life she lives is not always easy, and she is not perfect.

"My relationship with God is not a ladder to climb. It's more like navigating a spiral staircase."

One particularly trying day a couple of years ago, Sarah desperately needed God to help her feel loved and adored. At morning chapel, she prayed: *God, I need to know you love me today. Show me you love me.* After she walked out of the chapel, everywhere she went people held doors open for her. One guy at work brought puppies, and she played with them all day. People wanted to give her hugs.

"I don't believe in coincidences," Sarah says with a smile. "I think God was romancing me."

Allison (Copenbarger) Vance grew up on a farm in rural Blue Mound, Ill. She went to Taylorville High School, where she was editor of her high school newspaper. Knowing she wanted to pursue journalism, she applied to the University of Illinois at Urbana-Champaign. At Illinois, she wrote for the Daily Illini, buzz magazine and The News-Gazette. She also interned for the Decatur Herald & Review and St. Louis Magazine. It wasn't until taking Walt Harrington's class that she fell in love with narrative writing. "Sister Sarah" won third place for personality-profile writing in the 2011 Hearst Journalism Awards and first place in the 2011 Marian and Barney Brody Creative Feature Article Writing Awards. Currently, Vance is a writer at the University of Illinois and a freelance magazine journalist. She has been published in Coastal Living, St. Louis Magazine, Milwaukee Magazine and Indianapolis Monthly.

Photo by John Dixon/The News-Gazette

SLICES OF LIFE

12

"Least likely to succeed"

By Phil Johnson

Cutting hair in the barbershop no one ever expected him to own, Seon Williams entertains in frenzied, fluid motions. In front of him rests a client, to the left a ringing phone he will not answer, to the right, one of 30 or so visitors who stop by every day to show love.

The 42-year-old's 2008 black Mercedes-Benz SL 550 convertible, visible through the window behind him, sits parked out front of The Whip Hair Designs in Champaign. Newspaper clippings, plaques, neighborhood event fliers and funeral programs paint his walls. Photos of friends and family frame his faded mirror. A scissor cut here, a close shave there, and Williams steps back to admire his work.

Later today, he and his funeral director will take a body resting in his funeral home across town for cremation. He will also sell a family its first insurance policy. He will return to his shop intermittently for scheduled haircuts. He hopes to have time to attend tonight's Champaign City Council meeting.

But, right now, something he heard at church last Sunday has Williams reflecting on the meaning of real friendship. A razor wrapped in the long, thick brown fingers of his right hand waves side to side as he speaks.

"Pastor Johnson over at Jericho said if we just listen, we will see who our true friends are," he says as his soft brown eyes widen from ovals to circles as if to say, "Think about that." His eyes do that a lot.

The topic is critics, or as Williams calls them, "dreambusters."

"They everywhere, man. People always wanna doubt you. They see you doing well for yourself, and they feel insecure. They can't feel good for you and show you love. What I'm trying to do is provide an example and opportunities for others to succeed."

"Least likely to succeed." That's what he remembers an assistant principal and a teacher at Urbana High School calling him decades ago. He nearly believed them. Where does one of 22 siblings and half-siblings growing up in poverty on Hickory Street in Champaign find opportunity? The answer, for Williams, was the military. The summer of 1986, after his junior year of high school, Williams enlisted in delayed entry for the Army. In basic training at Fort Leonard Wood, Mo., that summer, he learned how to properly brush his teeth, make his bed and tie his shoes. The following summer he left for Fort Bragg, N.C. The next 6½ years sent Williams all around Europe. He liked how no one in the military cared about his background. The military cared only about solutions.

"I believe every young man should join the military," Williams says. "It shows you how to take control over your environment. It shows you how to be a game changer."

Williams wakes up every morning between 6:30 and 7 a.m.

"The first thing I do is praise God and then debrief with my wife," he says.

Debrief. An insurance agent/funeral director/barber needs a daily plan. When Williams opened The Whip in 1999, he saw it as a straight, steady job. He began cutting hair in the military and earned his barber's license from Concept College of Cosmetology in Urbana after he mustered out in 1994. His "Most Promising Graduate" plaque hangs on his shop wall.

He opened the shop with a $10,000 grant from Champaign's Community Collaboration for Economic Development. The grant specifically sought out black businessmen. He knows it took faith to open the shop with his limited education and limited resources. He envisioned a high-scale, high-volume barbershop. "Whip 'em in, whip 'em out," a friend told him. The name stuck, the idea did not. The demand wasn't there: 904 N. 4th St. in Champaign wasn't an up-scale, high-volume part of town.

"I began to think of it this way," Williams says. "If a customer does not have money to pay me, how am I going to pay the bills?"

Williams expanded his vision. He posted job openings in the shop. He told single mothers they could drop off their children for a haircut and pick them up after running errands. He cut hair for free in neighborhood parks during cookouts and in senior centers. "We even had a jar back in the day. It was for community members' prison commissaries." The Whip became a gathering place for a wide array of African Americans.

"I have professionals come in here for a haircut, and I have people come in who can't even spell the word 'professional,'" Williams says. "I see a barber's clientele as a reflection of self. You have to ride the elevator up and down. For me, that's easy. I have family like that."

By his 28th birthday, Seon Williams had lost five of his brothers. At age 6, he saw James, his 19-year-old brother, hang himself. It was just after church a few days before Christmas. He and his older siblings used to run upstairs in their old house on Beardsley Street in Champaign and compete to see who could change out of their Sunday school clothes the fastest, and the first one back downstairs won. Seon remembers losing that day to his brother, Joe. But when Seon got downstairs, Joe didn't brag. He stared. James was flailing. Seon and Joe ran to get help, but by the time they got back, it was too late.

"I wish I could have known better that day," Williams says. "But I was too young to understand what was going on."

Williams' mother, Roline Brumfield, moved the family out of the house after James died. Death followed. Brother Rap died from pneumonia. Gerald was shot and killed at an after-hours joint. Danny died in prison. Ricky fell victim to AIDS.

"When you grow up in poverty, pain is inevitable," Williams says. "For me, I just have to pray on it and move forward toward a solution."

In 2003, Williams opened a restaurant next door to his barbershop — "The Whip Café with a Taste of Soul." His mother served as head cook. It felt great, putting his mother to work in something they both loved.

On the café's first Thanksgiving, they served free dinners to hundreds. That year, Williams and his mother earned the Black Business of the Year Award from Champaign's Council of African-American Men. That plaque hangs on his barbershop wall, too. Williams sold the restaurant in 2006 when it became too much for his aging mother to handle.

In 2010, he opened Williams Memorial Services, after his best friend and workout partner, Antonio Monyeil Turner, collapsed and died of a heart attack. Williams organized his friend's funeral. After mourners praised his organization and attention to detail, he opened his own funeral home.

Twenty funerals into his business, Williams noticed a trend: Fifteen of the families he served were left without insurance. A few weekend classes later, Williams earned his insurance license.

Seon Williams wears his Sunday finest every day of the week. When he sits down a client, he hangs his coat jacket and works in a dress shirt and tie, dress pants and dress shoes. Several plastic wristbands adorn his right arm. One touts a fundraiser for The Church of The Living God.

A week ago, a friend stopped by selling wristbands for another church. They read "Dream, Drive, Team." He bought two. A 73-inch Sony flat-screen television dominates the center of The Whip, and clients can change the channel to whatever they want. That usually means sports. In Williams' corner sits his own television, a 40-inch Sanyo. He watches the morning shows. When the soaps start, he changes to CNN.

"I like staying current with the world," he says.

The recent Trayvon Martin coverage catches his eye.

"Isn't Trayvon the kid who got shot up in Chicago?" asks a client.

"It was down in Sanford, Fla.," Williams says.

And he wonders: Was Trayvon Martin ever labeled "least likely to succeed?"

Phil Johnson graduated from the University of Illinois in 2012 with a bachelor's degree in news-editorial journalism. He returned to Illinois the following year and received his master's degree in journalism. A Rockford, Ill., native, Phil spent three years writing opinion columns for the Daily Illini and a year working as the sports editor of The Spread, an online student magazine. He is currently interning in Manhattan as a sports writer for Business Insider. He also has interned at the Peoria Journal Star and the Rockford Register Star.

13

Becoming Christian

By Xing Zhuo

"Do you believe Jesus Christ is the son of God?" Elder Wei-Laung Hu asked.

"Yes, I do." Kaiwen Man answered.

"Do you accept Jesus as your savior and Lord in life?"

"Yes, I do."

"Will you follow Jesus our Lord as his loyal disciple?"

"Yes, I will."

Early on Easter morning this year, the minister at the Champaign Chinese Christian Church in Champaign supported Kaiwen by his back and immersed him in the church's baptismal tub. When he reemerged, Kaiwen stood straight, drenched and baptized, while his new brothers and sisters applauded. After only seven months in America, the 23-year-old Chinese student — an atheist all his life — had become a Christian.

"God saved me and my entire family," Kaiwen says. "I have to believe in Him."

Kaiwen's journey to belief began a few weeks after he arrived on the University of Illinois campus last August to earn his master's degree in economics. His neighbor, Lisa Liu, the wife of a Chinese post-doctoral student, invited him to Bible study at the Chinese Christian Church on a Friday night.

Kaiwen met some 35 Chinese students and non-students who attend the church regularly. They sang spirituals in Chinese, studied the Bible in English, ate snacks and chatted after finishing the last prayer of the evening.

Born and raised an atheist, Kaiwen didn't believe in such a thing as "prayer." For Kaiwen, the Bible was nothing more than a work of Western literature, something he had read simply because he wanted to improve his English.

"I read at the Bible in junior high school, but purely as a form of literature," he says. "When I was an exchange student in South Korea, we had some seminars on religion, also for discussion only." So he went to the service to practice

Photo by Darrell Hoemann/The News-Gazette

SLICES OF LIFE

his English. "But also because I feel like my heart needs it. I stayed and never have I missed one."

What exactly did his heart need? A religion? He never thought so before. A sense of belonging in a strange and foreign land? Maybe, but his master's program enrolls more than 90 percent international students, most of them Chinese. A chance to find peace and atone for his sins? Before entering the church doors, Kaiwen didn't even understand the word "sin."

So why did he become a Christian?

"It all came down to one question: Do you believe in yourself or the Bible?" he says. "Those signs and miracles that you didn't see, you cannot prove it right or prove it wrong with your own knowledge. Then do you believe it or not?

"I choose to believe the Bible."

Peter Chiligiris, one of only two Americans in the Chinese Church, leads Kaiwen's Bible study. He was a missionary in China for five years in the 1990s, and is now an English as a Second Language teacher at Illinois.

"Peter's words came with warmth and energy," Kaiwan says. "It was light. I enjoy listening to him talking about the Bible, and my faith wouldn't come that quick if Peter didn't share his own story with us, a family story that reminded me of my own. The Bible I've read, the words Peter told us, my thoughts after what I've experienced, and, of course, the kind of miracles happened on me and my family — I guess that's what made my belief."

At a regular Friday night Bible class last winter, Peter was leading Kaiwen's study group on Genesis 47, the chapter about Jacob's faith and his family.

"How can your faith affect your family?" Peter asked.

Peter then told the gathering that his father was a highly respected physician in his community, but he was also an alcoholic. When Peter became a Christian in his early 20s, he wrote his father a letter explaining why. When his father wrote back, he told his son that he had entered an alcohol rehabilitation program — and that he wanted to accept Jesus into his life, as Peter had done. He told his son, "This letter meant a great deal to me. It really changed my life."

Peter told the group, "When God asks you to do something, just do it. You never know what's gonna happen."

Kaiwen wept upon hearing Peter's story. He couldn't help it. The tears wouldn't stop. He thought of his own father, a college graduate, something rare in 1980s China. When Kaiwen was 12, his father started a company in Beijing. He brought Kaiwen with him there from their remote hometown in northwestern China and left Kaiwen's mother behind. Kaiwen was sent to a boarding school and returned home only on weekends. His father was always busy, often traveling for work. Kaiwen cooked for himself and spent most of his time alone.

Kaiwen never liked Beijing. As an outsider from a poor and remote province, he was mocked and bullied by his school roommates. He made few friends and spent most of his time reading — a favorite was Harry Potter, whom he thought of as a spiritual friend. Kaiwen didn't know why his father had brought him to Beijing only to abandon him. All he knew was that he was full of anger toward his father. Their relationship grew even more distant when Kaiwen went to college. His father's company wasn't doing well and he also had lost a lot of money in the stock market. His father was angry all the time. The fury was sometimes targeted at Kaiwen. Although his father paid Kaiwen's tuition and living expenses, that seemed to be the only thing between them. They seldom talked or communicated.

"But Peter's story reminded me of my own family, me and my father," Kaiwen says. "I started to think about how much I owe my parents. I think the Holy Spirit is helping me."

That was why he cried and cried and couldn't stop.

"The reason I could be here pursuing my dream is because of my parents' support. If not for the lessons I have from Peter — from God — I may not contact them anymore. My parents may spend the rest of their lives alone in China, living in misery. My father may lose everything in the stock market and fall seriously ill. My mother may follow that pattern. My family may be doomed."

Soon after that Bible class, at a Sunday morning worship, a congregant they call Aunt Qiao asked Kaiwen, "If you think of yourself as an innocent kid, there are delicious snacks in front of you, and you know it's good. Don't you want to taste it?"

Kaiwen asked himself, "You've read the Bible, and you know it's good. Why do you fear accepting it? Why set yourself apart from the true, the good and the beautiful?"

Aunt Qiao held Kaiwen's hands and prayed with him. At that moment, he made up his mind to become a Christian. Kaiwen also took Peter's advice and just did what he believed God was telling him to do. He called his parents, and he now does so often. He told them about his time in the United States, how he was changed because of what he learned at the church, and how he had become a Christian.

"You've grown up," his father said.

A cliché, yes, Kaiwen says, but a warm and loving sentiment still.

What does it mean to become a Chinese Christian? According to official numbers, about 20 million people in China are Christians. Unofficially, that number is probably double, even triple. Compared with the overall population of 1.3

billion, the Chinese Christian community is small regardless.

A Christian identity also brings obstacles in the atheist society. In theory, members of the China Communist Party should be atheists, which means Kaiwen will no longer qualify for party membership, a prerequisite for many of the best jobs in China. Being a Christian in China also means complying with government regulations and gathering only in designated churches.

Christians not registered with the Ministry of Civil Affairs, who gather in "family churches" in individual homes can earn government interference. For example, when Beijing's Shouwang Church, a "family church" made up primarily of intellectuals, tried to hold its Sunday prayer in public in 2009, some church leaders were placed under house arrest and remain so today.

Is Kaiwen prepared for that kind of life?

"I am not bothered," he says. "I want to stay here for longer time, and my parents don't object to that. Maybe someday I will bring them here."

Along with Kaiwen's conversion, good things have happened. His father recovered his losses in the stock market, closed his own company and got a new job as general manager in another competitor's firm. After a decade of separation, his mother moved to Beijing to be with his father. Kaiwen has never felt closer to them.

"God saved my family," he says.

But what if these good things had never happened?

"I would still believe in God," Kaiwen says. "Why? Because the Bible says so."

Xing Zhuo is originally from Ziyang, a small city in the southwestern part of China, 200 miles from where giant pandas were first found. In 2012, after finishing his undergraduate degrees in English and international studies in Beijing, he went on to pursue a master's degree in broadcast journalism at the University of Illinois. As a graduate student, he worked for the Daily Illini as a feature writer. He covered topics ranging from Korean pop star PSY to Chief Illiniwek. He has interned at several television stations and websites, working as a reporter, an assistant producer and as the guy rolling the teleprompter.

Photo by John Dixon/The News-Gazette

SLICES OF LIFE

14

The gunmen

By Gabrielle Irvin

The sooty, unpolished wood floor in Dave's Firearms hasn't been refinished in years. Laid with random planks of different widths and lengths, it stretches across the small shop, supporting thinly stocked shelves that hold Hodgdon's Longshot Powder and Blackhawk! holsters. Safely guarded in a smudged glass case are Nighthawk Dominator and Falcon pistols. Along the shop's back wall lean Winchester and Benelli shotguns.

Although Dave's Firearms, in the country outskirts of east Urbana, remains stocked with shotguns, shooting targets and camouflage rifle slings, President Obama's recent gun control proposals have triggered a surge of firearms and ammunition sales, leaving Dave Costley's ammo shelves nearly bare because gun owners are buying ammunition in bulk, fearful of new weapon control laws.

To 58-year-old Dave and the men who frequent his store, the proposals threaten a long-ingrained way of life. To these men, guns are at the heart of a culture deeply rooted in their lives — a culture of hunting and shooting for sport, of independence and camaraderie.

Dave, as well as Tieje Gaylord and Aaron Fruhling, regulars at the shop, load their own firearm cartridges and shotgun shells. They love hunting and sport shooting. They love the crispness of early morning air. They love the friendships they create.

"When I was young it was the fun of the hunt," says Tieje, a 46-year-old skeet shooter and hunter. "It still is, but there's more to it. It's havin' a bunch of guy friends who're interested in what you're interested in, and just havin' a good time." He also loves hanging out at Dave's, enjoys the banter and goofing.

"It's like a club," he says. "It's fun."

Dave is a large, balding man with gray hair and eyeglasses. As usual, today he wears beige cargo pants, brown leather Birkenstock work boots and a camouflage V-neck long-sleeved T-shirt. Before opening the gun shop in 2003, he simultaneously owned Sport 101, his first firearms store, and Wild Thang Cycles, a bicycle sales and repair shop in Urbana.

He figured that at 220 pounds he was destined to be a "way better shooter than a cyclist." He also couldn't find what he was looking for as a shooter: high-dollar sporting shotguns, sporting and trap reloading supplies, and specific firearms brands such as Caesar Guerini and Beretta. He thought, "Hell, this couldn't be too hard," and invested his money from the BMX business into a full-fledged firearms store.

"It's a passion to hunt or shoot competitions; to sell the guns is just a job," Dave says. "To me, to get up to go to work is OK. To get to go huntin' or shootin'? I'm up an hour before anybody, the alarm never has to be set."

Dave loves the competition and the cool morning breeze on his face. He enjoys the sounds of squawking feathered game. His shotgun is not just an accessory; it has become a part of him — a faint dark outline of the tip of his shotgun barrel is even imprinted on his right boot, where his gun rests when unloaded and broken open.

He was 12 when he got his first shotgun, a 20-gauge Mossberg. He'll always remember his first pheasant kill while hunting with his father, grandfather and uncle. It was the first time they had allowed him to carry a gun. As he walked slowly through the cornstalks, a pheasant flushed from under his feet and cackling its distinct, shrill cry.

"Shoot it!" his father hollered.

"I remember lifting the gun up, thinking, 'Man, that's a cool noise,' and BOOM, shot the bird."

Dave's Firearms smells of Gus, Dave's 9-year-old yellow Labrador, of gun oil and aging wood. The checkout counter shelves are cluttered with firearms catalogs, old boxes of bullets and a hair-filled wooden dog brush. A gray trash can — decorated with brown coffee stains and chewing tobacco spit — stands tall behind the counter. From his stool behind that counter, Dave watches customers, talks bull with Tieje and Aaron, and feeds leftover treats to Gus. Except for BBQ, that is. It gives Gus gas really bad, mind-numbingly bad.

"Gus has always been very popular," says Aaron, a 53-year-old hunter and trap and skeet shooter. A short, bald man with a neatly trimmed goatee, camouflage pants and a blue Ameren sweatshirt, Aaron got his first BB gun when he was 10. At 14, he got his first shotgun, a Savage 12-gauge. He grew up on a farm in Ogden Township, where he and his family still gather on Easter and get the clay bird thrower out. He bought his son a 20-gauge shotgun when he was 10 years old.

"He'd shoot that gun till his cheek was purple," Aaron laughs, referring to the shotgun's bruising kick back when not seated just right on a person's shoulder.

He and Tieje shoot targets and hunt coyote and pheasant together. They've known each other for years and enjoy hunting coyote at their spot near Potomac.

"We always have a blast jokin' around and walkin'," Aaron says. Tieje helped Aaron remodel his kitchen. "And it's a pretty nice kitchen," Aaron says.

Aaron peruses Dave's near-empty ammo shelves and leans on the counter near the cash register.

"Hey, Dave, do you have any XD(M) clips?" he asks, looking to stock up on magazines for his Springfield XD(M) 9mm pistol.

"No."

"Expecting to get any anytime?"

"I'm hoping at some point and time, yeah," Dave replies with uncertainty.

"OK, if you get one —"

"Set one aside for ya'?"

"Tell Tieje or something 'cause he's in here more than I am," Aaron jokes.

"I ain't tellin' him," Dave kids back. "He'll buy it for 20 bucks and sell it to you for 40."

"Nah, he treats me pretty good," Aaron says, actually serious for a change.

Tieje is a youthful man with short brown hair and a goatee. He sits on a stool at the counter and dangles his brown boots above the floor.

"I stop in here all the time," he says. "My wife gets off work two hours later than I do, and my girls are both grown up, so I stop in here and I hang out for a couple hours and go home."

At age 11, Tieje hunted raccoon, pheasant and rabbit with a middle-school buddy and his father. It was the thrill that hooked him: the thrill of trudging through the weeds, finding a quarry, having it jump and scurry or fly away. He bought his first brand-new gun, a Remington 870 12-gauge, when he was 19. He still shoots it when he goes pheasant hunting.

"It's not a fancy gun," he says. "I just like it. It's light. It's what I shoot the most as far as for hunting, and every time I pick it up it's the same thing. It's there. It's always there every fall when I go to get it out, and it's ready to go. It's the first one I bought, and I'll never get rid of it."

Dave, Tieje and Aaron load their own rifle cartridges and shotgun shells. "Custom load building," Dave calls it. The men want precision. Dave loads specifically for his two .25 Winchester rifles. He controls the bullet weight, power charge and seating depth.

"If something screws up, it's nobody else's fault but mine," Dave says. "When I go shoot and I shoot a good score, it's because of me."

Tieje has a gun in his hand every weekend during the summer. He competes in sporting clays shooting competitions alongside his 21-year-old daughter, whom the men call "Darling Sarah." She began skeet shooting when she was about 15. Dave sold her her first shotgun and also employs her in the shop whenever she needs extra cash. Her high school senior picture — a black-and-white photo of her holding a shotgun and wearing a camouflage T-shirt — hangs on the wall near the checkout counter.

"Every time I come in here I learn something," Tieje says as he sits with Dave behind the counter. "I don't want to admit it, but I learn something. Not only do I consider Dave my friend, but the people who are in here my friends. It's neat to see guns come in and go out, and I pay attention to what they're talkin' about and I'm learnin', too. That's what's cool about this place. It's 'Cheers.' It's kinda like 'Cheers' with guns."

Dave considers the comparison to the once-popular barroom TV sitcom, laughs and agrees.

"It is a lot like that."

Gabrielle Irvin is from Grass Valley, Calif., a rural town in the western foothills of the Sierra Nevada mountain range. She graduated from the University of Nevada, Reno in 2012 with a bachelor's degrees in journalism and political science. She graduated from the University of Illinois in 2013 with a master's degree in news-editorial journalism. She currently blogs for Synergy HomeCare of Inland Empire SW, a nonmedical in-home care company in Corona, Calif. She has also worked as a communications intern for the Department of Electrical and Computer Engineering at the University of Illinois, a writer for The Union and a marketing intern for Big Brothers Big Sisters of Northern Nevada. Her favorite journalist is Pete Earley. His story, Missing Alice, encouraged her to write a self-reported investigation of her brother's life and death. In her spare time, she enjoys swimming, playing softball and indulging in ridiculous dramatic television shows.

Gabrielle Irvin

15

Never give up

By Candice Norwood

The Rev. Ervin Williams loves Sunday night, the rare time when he can stop, relax and listen. As the founder of Champaign's Restoration Urban Ministries, his work week is long and often divided among preaching three church services, running staff meetings and teaching classes aimed at helping the 120 homeless residents the ministry has on average in its Transitional Housing Program.

Yet each Sunday, he and a handful of congregants gather inside Restoration's sanctuary for worship and testimony. During the morning service, the sanctuary's 60 chairs might be full. Tonight, there are 14 people.

Sitting in the front row near the center aisle, Williams wears a navy blue suit, V-neck dress shirt and worn, black leather shoes. A strikingly calm, soft-spoken man, he often appears tired and older than his 62 years. He sits quietly, in concentration, with his head tilted toward the sky, his eyes squinting.

He listens as a former resident of the housing program talks about the sense of community she felt at Restoration. He listens to Bonnie Craft-Tolston, with tears rolling down her face, as she thanks God for getting her through hardships.

When Williams makes his way up to the church stage, there's a slight limp in his walk, the result of nerve damage that has weakened the left side of his body.

"When we worship tonight something's got to chant in you: 'Behold the eyes of the Lord,'" he tells the gathering, a hint of southern Missouri twang still in his voice. "You won't see judgment; you see love and passion. There's something in those eyes that says, 'I won't give up on you. I won't give up.'"

After all, Williams knows people did not give up on him. Not as he struggled to create his ministry, not when he was ravaged by drugs and drink, and not when he was a boy living in Smelterville. That wasn't the official name for the small annex to Cape Girardeau, Mo., between La Cruz Street on the north end and Cape La Croix Creek on the south, but the nickname stuck for Williams' home neighborhood. Bordered by outhouses, backwoods and a rock quarry, Smelterville gained a reputation as the "dumping place for all the poor," he says.

Photo by Bradley Leeb/The News-Gazette

He can still remember the heavy scent of gasoline from the neighborhood's mobile tanks. When it wasn't gas in the air, it was sewage from the city facility nearby. When it wasn't sewage, it was "chitlins" — pig intestines — from the meat processing plant.

"We'd go to school smelling like whatever the flavor of the air was that day because it would be in our clothing," he says. "Everybody washed. We were clean, but they had the smell."

Growing up, Williams, his mother and 11 siblings all lived in his grand-mother's home. His grandma was a hard-working, Christian woman, who taught Williams the value of helping others. She visited the sick and cleaned their hous-es — just because she wanted to help. She used the little money she made scrub-bing floors to get Williams piano lessons and the clothing he needed to be an altar boy at their African Methodist Episcopal Church.

Other than summer visits to his biological father, a minister in Champaign, Williams didn't have a man to look up to in his life until he was 5 and his mother married his stepdad. He encouraged the boy's curiosity and told him he "needed to do something" with his life. Williams called him Daddy.

Each Christmas, the boys in his family traditionally got cowboy hats and toy guns so they could mimic their favorite TV cowboys. When Williams was 10, however, he wanted a microscope instead. He didn't have the heart to tell his fam-ily. He knew they were poor and didn't have the money for such a gift. Yet, when he unwrapped his present on Christmas day, he found a microscope — a gift from Daddy. Talking about it today still brings tears to his eyes.

"I could never figure out how my stepdad knew what I wanted was a micro-scope," he says. "That was something that changed my whole life."

Even as a child, Williams was a leader. He joined the Boy Scouts at 12 and read books constantly. His favorites were comic books and biographies — the stories of great men imagined and real. At 17, he rallied his friends and created a civic center for Smelterville, where kids could hang out, stay out of trouble and train for jobs. After two years as a paramedic for the Army in his early 20s, Williams attended Eastern Illinois University, where he graduated with a degree in psychology.

In 1976, he moved to Oklahoma City with his new wife Marilyn to manage a Sears department store. After a couple of years, he left Sears and set up his own businesses, first a general goods store, then a carpentry company. When the businesses took off, the money started coming in. For the first time, Williams could afford nice houses, cars, clothing and security for his family. He couldn't stop working or slow down. He wanted more.

Many moments were good. One day, he and Marilyn were so excited about their prosperity that they went to the bank, brought home a large number of single bills and tossed them in the air for fun. Afterward, they neatly stacked the bills again and returned them to the bank.

But then came the drugs: alcohol, marijuana and cocaine. At first, he could control them. But slowly, they took over his life. Williams didn't have his grandmother's religion to fall back on. By then, he had become an agnostic.

It all came to a head at age 28. He was sitting in his truck outside a motel where his crew was working. Drunk and high, the music blasting — Williams is hazy on the details today — his car "somehow" changed gears from park to drive and ran a hole right through the building. The insurance company wouldn't cover the damage, so $50,000 had to come from his pocket.

Williams started "going through money like tissue paper," as he puts it, and was forced to shut down his offices. Tension at home got to be too much, and he moved to a motel, leaving Marilyn alone for three months to care for their young son. He wanted to give up. He saw nothing going his way. Then a friend insisted he and Marilyn come to a service at the friend's small Baptist church. Williams was reluctant but knew that he didn't have much to lose.

Stepping into the church that day felt like "coming home," he remembers. A sense of freedom came over him. At this church, a woman they called Mother Towns told him that God had called on her to help guide Williams and Marilyn back to Him. Everyday after work they would go to Mother Towns' home to pray — sometimes for two or three hours.

"She would just tell me: 'You're almost there, you need to pray a little longer. You're almost there.'"

And he would dutifully pray some more. Mother Towns wouldn't give up on him. Weeks with her turned into months, and when Williams opened his first ministry in Oklahoma City a couple of years later, Mother Towns came.

She looked Williams in the eye and said: "You're my pastor now."

The ministry started out small — a gathering of friends praying together — but it grew quickly. Then, just after Williams had moved his congregation to a larger facility, he got an unexpected phone call from his father in Champaign. He was sick with diabetes and needed help with his own ministry. So in 1989, he and Marilyn moved. As his father's health deteriorated, though, so did his ministry. Williams began putting Restoration together.

In its early years, Restoration Ministries was a food and clothing pantry until Williams purchased an old motel and created the housing program in 1997.

His work at Restoration is never easy. It's a constant fight to win small battles: help a resident get a job or kick a drug addiction. Williams knows that he can't save everyone, but he lives for the days when he can get through to just one person — a person such as Tiffany Walton, a single mother of five who came to Restoration last June defeated, with gambling and alcohol abuse problems.

Today, she's sober and has hopes of going to cosmetology school.

Williams' goal is to provide people with skills that can make them independent. He can't do it alone. His efforts are fueled by the faith of the community members who provide the $480,000 yearly that Restoration needs on average to keep running. Some days this faith arrives as a $20 bill, which Bishop King James Underwood of the New Free Will Baptist Church drops off from time to time. Other days it comes as the $250,000 or $750,000 checks Williams says someone once sent anonymously with instructions to expand the facility.

Restoration reached its 20th anniversary recently, and Williams can't help but think about his years with the ministry. One afternoon inside the living room of his quaint, two-story home in north Champaign, he sits in an armchair smiling as he talks about the future. His body has slowed, and he has cut back hours at the ministry due to back pain and recent neck surgery. In a few years, it will be time to pass on the leadership.

"I have to leave so that a new person or group of people can continue to make Restoration grow and evolve into what it is supposed to be."

He wants to spend more time with Marilyn — just the two of them. Maybe they'll move to Tennessee where they have family, or maybe they'll just stay in Champaign and enjoy each other's company.

Williams eases out of his chair and walks gingerly to his front lawn. It's a nice, spring day. He lifts his head to take in the sun. He often thinks about what Restoration will become without him. He knows it will be different once he's gone.

"But that's OK," he says. "It's their time."

Candice Norwood is a St. Louis native. She followed in her father's footsteps by majoring in news-editorial journalism at the University of Illinois. Her media experience includes writing and editing for The Daily Illini, Her Campus Illinois and IMPULSE magazine. She also has interned at the St. Louis American, the San Diego Union-Tribune and Newsday. After graduating in 2013 with a bachelor's degree in journalism and a minor in Spanish, Candice will spend a year working as an English teaching assistant in Madrid. She has visited 12 countries and hopes to incorporate her interests in journalism, travel and language into a career. In her free time, Candice can be found blogging, tweeting about pop culture and politics, or cooking. She dedicates this story to her parents, Ronald and Kimberly Norwood: the people who taught her to "never give up."

Photo of Connie Bickers by John Dixon/The News-Gazette

SLICES OF LIFE

16

The human cost

By Jonathan Jacobson

Connie Bickers gave me simple directions to her house in St. Joseph, but the country roads in central Illinois all look the same and in the pitch black of a winter evening I get lost. I find her house when I see a memorial road sign labeled "Cory Hubbell Way." The sign was dedicated last October by Illinois Lt. Gov. Pat Quinn in honor of Bickers' son, who died while serving in Kuwait in 2003. He is the reason I'm here.

"Can I show you Cory's room?" Connie asks, leading me into a space filled floor to ceiling with memorabilia from her son's life. Awards and recognitions, his Army boots and his uniforms, an old football he tossed around in the desert signed by members of his unit, memorial quilts knitted by military mothers to honor his service, and Connie's collection of at least 30 angels that she began assembling after Cory's death at 20 years old.

"He was my angel," she says, fighting back tears.

They come in pairs. Always two of them to soften the blow. Sometimes they arrive early in the morning, waiting in the driveway for the first light to come on in the house. Two young soldiers, hair cropped tight against their skin. They have appeared at nearly 4,000 homes across America in this way to tell families that a son or daughter will not be returning home from the Iraq war.

So many dead, many of them about my age, 22. Yet I know not a single one of them, not a single family member who has lost a child. I have not even known a friend who lost a friend. In one of America's most controversial wars, I have been a spectator. There is a picture of me in a suburban Chicago newspaper from my sophomore year of high school. I stand self-righteously behind a bed-sheet banner that reads "No War." I was 16 when the U.S. invaded Iraq, barely tall enough to be seen over our high school lobby declaration.

What did I really know?

So a few months ago, I vowed to change that. I drew a circle around

Champaign-Urbana and collected the names of the soldiers who had died within about a 70-mile radius. I found about 10. I set out to visit their homes and their families, their friends and their neighbors. I wanted to see and feel the way this war has changed the people it has left behind. For me and for so many others like me who have lived the war through newspaper headlines and television clips, I set out to understand the human cost of war.

Some people I called asked that I never call them again. Others had moved out of the area since their soldiers' deaths, and I was unable to reach them. Ultimately, I found five families who agreed to sit down and talk about life after death. In living rooms, in restaurants, in cemeteries and at memorial sites, I met the people whose lives were forever altered by the day those two soldiers appeared at their door.

Time has not healed Connie Bickers' wounds.

"It's like every year it's just a little bit worse," she says. "I don't know if it's that reality is setting in because you know they're not coming home... It will be five years this year, and I'm starting to face reality that it's never going to happen"

Connie is a small woman with short, wheat-colored hair. Walking through her home, she tries to read a framed letter her son wrote her from Kuwait. But her voice won't push through the tears and she leans back against a wall to support herself. She cries nearly every day, she says. Every day for five years, nearly 2,000 days of tears. She says that, for her, it's best not to pay attention to the war.

"I don't watch TV, I don't watch the news, I don't read the newspapers for that reason," she says. "Because every time I think about it, you just think about how another family feels the same pain that we are."

A humble stone memorial in the front yard sits in the chilly evening, guarded by an American flag whipping in the wind. Connie walks to it and lights a cigarette, hugging her arms against her body to keep warm. She gestures toward the dirt surrounding the memorial and takes a last drag.

"In the spring, there'll be red, white and purple petunias," she says.

Good luck finding Sandy and Kevin Cawvey's home in Mahomet, where all roads signs read "County Road" and come complete with some barely legible numbers that allegedly distinguish one from another. Farm equipment rests on the lawns of homes and decaying hay accumulates in front of one farmhouse.

Sitting in their comfortable living room with a view of the snow thawing in the 5-acre backyard, Sandy and Kevin talk about a promise their daughter, Jessica — then a 20-year-old Army National Guard soldier – made when she came home on leave from Iraq in June of 2004. She pinkie-swore to her 5-year-old daughter,

Sierra, that she would not die.

"Mommy, pinkie swear you won't die," little Sierra said. Jessica looked desperately at her mom as if to say, "Don't make me do this."

"Just pinkie swear you won't die," Sandy told Jessica.

On the couch tonight, Sandy pauses. "After it did happen that she did die, I could kind of see why she wouldn't want to do it."

Alhough her grandparents had been heavily involved in raising Sierra — Jessica was 15 when her daughter was born — they took over as full-time parents that day. Sierra has sandy blond hair pulled tight to her head. She is thin and short for her age — the smallest on her entire basketball team — but her energy is palpable.

"We probably give her more than we gave our kids," says Kevin.

"We love her more," Sandy says, laughing.

Unlike Connie Bickers — and, in fact, unlike all the other families I meet — the Cawveys don't cry in front of me. But their poise is hard-earned. After hearing about her daughter's death, Sandy says, "I cried for a million years, right Sierra?"

"You didn't cry for a million years," Sierra says, smiling at the loving game they have made from the tragedy. "You cried for a billion years."

Jessica was killed when a bomb exploded beneath her truck on Oct. 6, 2004. Her father, who drives a truck for Aramark Uniforms, took three weeks off after her death. But when he returned to work, he found that when he was behind the wheel, he pictured Jessica driving her truck through the desert.

"I think of her often," he says. "Driving trucks myself, a lot of times just driving down the road, I'm thinking what it must have been like for her when it hit."

He speaks slowly and carefully. It seems to hurt him physically when he talks about his daughter, and he falls quiet. Sandy carries the conversation, stepping into Kevin's occasional silences with other stories about her daughter. She says attending church has been difficult for them since Jessica died.

"We kind of felt like God could have protected her and instead He didn't," Sandy says. "And we don't know why. We just don't know why He took our baby."

The Cawveys are frustrated with the way the war has been run, and they believe the U.S. soldiers in Iraq should come home. Sandy doesn't need encouragement to share her opinion.

"I don't know if I ever was angry," she says. "I'm not angry at the Iraqi people… Somebody's babies from over there are getting killed. Their regular people are getting killed every day. I want all the people to come home right now. Absolutely."

For some reason, this response surprises me. I expect to hear "gung-ho" rhetoric about finishing what we started from someone who has lost so much to the cause. I expect to hear that these people want their daughter's death avenged by more death and a U.S. victory. But the only thing Kevin and Sandy want is for the war to end.

Eventually, the Cawveys take me to a small room filled with Jessica's mementos — old photos, awards and a portrait an Iraqi drew of her — as well as a grand piano. With Sierra playing staccato notes in the background, Sandy points out her favorite photos. Many were taken in the old house closer to the town where they lived until two years ago. One is the last picture Jessica took with her daughter, on an airport tarmac at 5 a.m. in July 2004, the day she left for Iraq.

"This is her last kiss that she gave her," Sandy says, pointing to the photo of Jessica kissing Sierra in the dark of the early morning. Some of the childhood pictures of Jessica look so incredibly similar to Sierra that I have to hold back asking which one is which.

"Sierra has the personality that Jessica developed," Sandy says. "Sierra is just like her mother was when she died."

Both before and after her 25-year-old son was killed in Iraq, Ava Tomson made quilts. She worked with a group called Marine Comfort Quilts, which sends 30-patch blankets to the surviving family members of Marines killed in the war. She expanded the group's operation to include other military branches like the Army, of which her son Lucas Starcevich — Ava's first husband's surname — was a member. All the newspaper obituaries point this out, so I'm familiar with Ava's hobbies long before I show up at her doorstep on a drizzly Monday evening. Her home is in Tolono, which she says is so small as to make inexcusable my cartographic shortcomings.

"If I decide to ride a bicycle," she says, "I can be across town in no time."

Ava has short brown hair, with highlights barely visible in the dimly lit interior of her orderly home. Light gray eyes lie behind glasses that hang in the middle of her nose, late-shift librarian-style. Her son died April 16, 2007. It's been barely a year.

"There is a, I don't know how to phrase it, there's a dead spot in your heart," she says, tears streaking her cheeks. "Like a big hole's been cut in it."

Ava is unashamed of her tears and doesn't try to hide them.

She takes me to her sewing operation, in a corner of the basement, next to an armoire that contains pictures, awards and other memorabilia from Lucas' life. Multicolored spools send thin strands of string through a state-of-the-art sewing machine connected to a computer. Ava has put together many quilts here in honor of America's soldiers, but she takes out the one that hurt the most, the quilt that her group presented to her in Lucas' memory.

"I can remember I had actually physically handled hundreds of those," she says. "It's one quilt you treasure but you never want to receive." She struggles to finish these words.

When I ask to see some of Lucas' old letters, she takes me into her bedroom and we sit cross-legged on her floor, speaking quietly as if there were someone in the house to overhear our private conversation. There is not. Ava's husband, Rick, drives a truck five days a week up north, and her sons are out for the evening. Amid the quiet, she says one of the things she misses most about her son is his smell. She is a bit embarrassed, although I tell her not to be. She then confides that she keeps some of his stuffed animals in a plastic bag to preserve his fragrance. She also hasn't washed some of the dirty clothes that came home after he died.

"They weren't stinky, but it was kind of a blessing because some of them still smell like him," she says. "And I guess it's a strange thing. You get to missing him terribly, and I just go down and I pull out that hat that he wore a lot or something and I can smell him and still feel close to him."

Then we sit in silence, hovering over the paper trail of Ava's son, crowded in the empty house.

Ed and Susan Miller's house in Oakwood is hard to miss. A fading American flag is painted on the barn next to it. They greet me at the door, and I immediately see on their refrigerator a picture of their nephew, Matthew Dillon, clad in full Marine regalia.

They introduce me to Susan's father, Norman Ponder, a thin man now grieving both for his grandson, who died in Iraq on Dec. 11, 2006, and his wife, who died a few weeks ago. Matt's immediate family used to live in central Illinois but moved to South Carolina about 20 years ago. The two families maintain close contact, speaking via telephone nearly every day.

The loss still feels very new in this home. It is on the refrigerator and in the family pictures, and it is in Norman's face.

"Hardly a day passes that you don't think about him," Norman says slowly, his words slurring together as if his lips were fighting to remain closed. "I walk down at the mall and, quite frequently, I see the Marines down there. It's just something that every time you see them on television, pictures of the boys over there, it's just a constant reminder that, uh .."

His voice fades, his eyes begin to water. Norman stands, pushing his chair back from the table, and walks out of the dining room without another word. In the living room, he grips the wall for support.

I am embarrassed to intrude on his private moment, the fragility of this family's psyche, even years after Matt's death.

When Norman leaves, Susan, her hands steepled over the wood table, and Ed hardly flinch. Susan looks away from her father, as if she's worried he will see her, and Ed quickly fills the gap in conversation. The Millers talk about Matt and his brother as children, their love of hunting and fishing. Ed is an outdoorsman and when the kids came over, they didn't sit around watching television.

"I took the boys fishing down here in a local pond, and we had a little boat out there," Ed says. "Next thing I knew I had a hook in my back and I go, 'We're done, pull it out and let's go.'" He and Susan laugh, but Ed's standard reticent expression soon returns.

When conversation turns to the war, it's clear that Ed holds stronger beliefs than his wife. Neither believes the U.S. should withdraw its troops from Iraq now. But Ed believes the war was a mistake from the beginning.

"I had no idea why we went to Iraq," he says, a hint of irritation in his voice. "I don't think they should have ever went there."

Susan, who attends church weekly without Ed, is more reserved in her judgment: "I think most people that are God-fearing people just hope and pray that they've done the right thing and pray that the war ends."

Both believe that Matt's choice to join the war was his own; no one forced it upon him.

"He had, in his heart, a job to do, and he did his job," Susan says.

Mark and Candy Spencer live in Sullivan, in a house surrounded by a beautiful green army of pine trees. They only recently moved out here, running from the memories that lived in their old house in neighboring Gays. Their son, Cole, died April 28, 2007 — only a few days after Ava's son, Lucas — when a bomb exploded beneath his Humvee near an al-Qaeda training facility.

Mark is a tall, muscular man — he was in the Air Force for five years — with blond, thinning hair and a yellow goatee. He speaks through his bassy, country-twang voice in short sentences. On the day of Cole's funeral, he says, two factories in Sullivan stayed closed so the workers could attend.

"All the workers were out in the road," he says. "It really made you feel good about your country."

But the loss of his 21-year-old son was hard to grasp.

"If you lose somebody that quick, you just can't believe it," he says. "When it happens to you, you're never ready. Even today, you don't really accept it because life is so valuable and so precious."

They had to leave the house where Cole grew up.

"I was just sitting on the bed crying, just looking at his room," Candy says, her head resting in her hands. "Every day until we moved. So it made it very rough to be in the house."

The Spencers, the Cawveys and the Bickerses have all moved out of their old family homes. Connie Bickers doesn't think that's coincidence. "Memories," she said, and that was that.

The Spencers take me to the cemetery where Cole is buried a few miles from their home. On the drive, Mark talks about fishing and deer hunting with Cole and their other son, Brian, who is 17. He points out the window to the places they liked to hunt and mentions the bucks he and Cole shot the year before he left for the Army. At Cole's grave, wind blows strong across the wide-open cemetery. Connie cleans off some dirt and leaves by the headstone. She and her husband talk about Brian, who rarely speaks about Cole. They say Brian feels some bitterness toward Muslims in the wake of his brother's death. They don't disagree.

"I will say I'm very anti any of them living over here in the United States," Candy says.

"I don't know what their motivations are," Mark adds, "but they're not American motivations."

Mark says it's time to go, and we pile into the car, heading back to their home.

On my way back home from each family's house, I rode in complete silence, winding my way through their beliefs and their pain. They have so much in common — they are among the thousands of families in America who have shouldered the ultimate cost of Iraq — but their responses to the war have been very different. Connie Bickers tunes Iraq out; the Cawveys believe it's time to remove the troops; the Spencers want to keep fighting until the mission's accomplished; the Millers think the war was a mistake from the beginning. Yet all their responses to this loss have been painfully similar. No relief, not really. I could never have learned that from behind my "No War" bed-sheet banner.

There was a war. There is a war. Ask Connie, Sandy and Kevin, Ava, Ed and Susan and Norman, and Mark and Candy. Unlike me and most of you, they are not spectators to Iraq.

Jonathan Jacobson was born in Chicago, Ill. He graduated from the University of Illinois in 2008, majoring in English and rhetoric. During college, he worked at the Daily Illini as a reporter, columnist and metro news editor. He also wrote for buzz magazine and the Arlington Heights Daily Herald and worked at the University's radio station, WPGU. He currently goes to Northwestern University School of Law and expects to graduate in 2014.

Photo by Heather Coit/The News-Gazette

SLICES OF LIFE
92

17

Missing the music

By Sonia Kurniawan

If only ...
If only he were back in Bali. He would not have so many sleepless nights. His heart would not ache with sadness because of his inability to infuse the feeling of his beloved gamelan music into the hearts of his American students.

"How am I to make my students one with the music?" he has asked himself constantly.

If only ...

That has been the lingering question since I Ketut Gede Asnawa, now a music instructor at the University of Illinois, moved to the United States nearly 13 years ago. Blinded by work stress and the feeling of not belonging, he could not always see that his move saved a very precious life.

"I don't know what would have happened if I hadn't moved," he says. "Thinking about it now, it scares me."

Asnawa was born in 1955 in Denpasar, Bali, Indonesia. He was a farmer's son and the seventh of 10 children. Bali, home to most of Indonesia's Hindu minority, is renowned for its arts, including Balinese dance, sculpture, painting, leather, metalworking — and the gamelan.

As a boy, Asnawa did not have the luxury of PlayStations, Nintendo Wiis or Xboxes. Instead, the young Asnawa found entertainment in nature and music. He played in the paddy fields, fished for catfish and scared the ducks. He reclined atop of bales of hay at the rice granary and stared at the night sky until sleep became too tempting to resist.

With this bucolic life came the Balinese gamelan — a traditional Indonesian orchestra collection of bronze percussion instruments. Asnawa's first taste of the gamelan came at age 7. Young and curious, he experimented with the ensemble: gongs, metallophones composed of a larger pair (ugal) and a smaller male-female pair (gangsas), chime gongs (reongs), and palm-sized cymbals (ceng-cengs). He also toyed with the double-sided membrane drum (kendang), which functions as the orchestra's rhythm keeper and plays the role of the baton in western classical music. The gamelan instruments are made and owned by the community, not individuals.

Asnawa's neighbor was a gamelan musician and had a small gamelan set at his house. He always welcomed Asnawa in to play. Playing the gamelan is second nature to Balinese children, but Asnawa stood out. He could listen to interlocking layers of the gamelan music — the ting-a-ling chime noises of the ceng-cengs or the shimmery ringing of the reongs — and then easily imitate their beats.

He loved the fiery side of gamelan music, filled with racing beats and intricate rhythms. To him, the gamelan was like a feisty child in broad daylight: playful, spontaneous and loud, a contrast to his quiet, polite and reserved nature. Seeing his talent, his uncle took him to the local bale, where the community gamelans are kept, for lessons.

"If you can play the gamelan well," Asnawa says of life in Bali, "you should offer yourself to the act of learning the gamelan. It's like a religious duty. The art of the gamelan is a part of worship to please the gods."

Gamelan musicians are well-respected figures in Balinese culture. They play a critical role in sustaining Balinese tradition, especially if they're musicians of Asnawa's caliber. A pioneer in contemporary gamelan, he has written books about the gamelan and is well-respected among Bali's 3.1 million residents. In Bali, he's a celebrity; in the United States, he is unknown.

Room 1188 of the Music Building starts to vibrate in rhythm to the beating of the drum, the shimmering of the gangsas, the booming of the gongs, and the clanging of the ceng-cengs. Asnawa's gamelan class is now in session.

"One, one, two, two, one, one, two, two, por, por, three, three, por, por ..." Asnawa's distinctly accented voice rises above the din as he counts to the beating of his drum. "Slow down, Peter!" Asnawa tells a student who brings down his mallet onto the reong a moment too soon.

"One, two, three, por, em — parang!" Asnawa says, as he tries to guide Peter by making his voice mimic the reong's sound. "One, two, three, four ..."

"You're still too fast, Peter!"

Peter's confusion is not unusual among Asnawa's American students. They lack "wirasa": the natural spirit, spontaneity and feel of gamelan music that the Balinese people seem to innately grasp and embody. Perhaps it would be like trying to teach the Balinese western classical, Cajun or Appalachian folk music that is culturally foreign to them. His American students are so focused on getting the notes right that they forget to listen. He wants his students to be able to shed their studied individualistic behavior and listen, reciprocate and play as part of a community.

"Why am I here in America, if I can't get them to play right?" Asnawa asks.

Asnawa had planned to be a gamelan professor at the music conservatory in Bali. Yet, despite his high stature, life as a teacher and gamelan musician in Indonesia can be hard — and wages are low. So, in 2003, when he was offered a Gamelan teaching position as a visiting professor at the University of Missouri-Kansas City Conservatory of Music, he took it. He uprooted his wife and two children from Bali and moved to the U.S. with hopes of a more materially prosperous future.

Soon, he received a terrible surprise.

Asnawa had long noticed that daughter Ni Made Yunirika's right shoulder was higher than her left, but he brushed if off, thinking that it was nothing serious. When he moved to the U.S., though, he took her to Kansas City's Children Mercy hospital for a check-up. The diagnosis: Yunirika, now 20, had scoliosis. If left untreated, the spinal issues would cause her serious problems and perhaps even death due to organ damage. Yunirika has had three operations and constant check-ups since the diagnosis. Asnawa knows that if he had stayed in Bali, she would likely be crippled. Today, she is healthy.

"I'm very grateful that I moved to the U.S.; if not, Yuni would suffer later," he says.

Yet Asnawa has struggled to adapt to American culture, which he sees as individualistic, high-strung and outspoken, unlike the more conservative, leisurely and collective culture of Bali. He misses Bali. He misses his friends. He misses playing the gamelan with his fellow countrymen — the interlocking beats and the spontaneity of the performance. The feistiness of the gamelan music in Bali is dulled here in America.

The feeling of wirasa is missing.

Asnawa's house in Urbana is a statement of his longings. Inside his two-story home, a faint smell of sandalwood permeates the air. It originates from an incense stick placed on a small basket made with coconut palm leaves — a typical Balinese offering.

"It's to ward off evil spirits and a gift to the gods," Asnawa says.

The alabaster-colored walls are lined with hand-carved wooden masks and various shadow puppets called wayangs that normally accompany gamelan performances. A large painted canvas depicts the story of Ramayana, a Balinese epic. Asnawa is particularly fond of this painting, which depicts Bali's native wayang characters.

"It's a rare painting, this one. It can only be obtained at the Kamasan Village in the north of Bali."

Pictures of family and friends from back home adorn the fridge. In his living room is a small gamelan set, where he and his children sometimes play for guests.

"This house is a place where I can feel at home and be myself."

Asnawa knows his students fall short of grasping the feeling of wirasa. But, for the benefits to his family, he has made his peace. He patiently teaches his students one mallet hit at a time, hoping to at least instill in them: "Magguru, Panggul dan Kuping" — roughly translated, it means to learn by watching and listening.

After all the years in America, Asnawa is grateful.

"That's the funny thing about life. You'll never know where it will take you," he says.

He doesn't regret moving: "I'll do it all over again if I have to."

Yet he also knows he won't be truly content until he returns home to his beloved Bali. Asnawa closes his eyes and sighs.

Yes, he will definitely return home. Just when, he is not sure, probably after his daughters finish their college degrees.

"I'm definitely coming back home."

Sonia Kurniawan was born in Jakarta, Indonesia. She majors in broadcast journalism, with a minor in business, at the University of Illinois. On the weekends, she works as a radio DJ for WPGU 107.1 FM, a student-run radio station. She also hosts her own specialty show on Monday nights called "Alternative Around the World." She took Walt Harrington's feature writing class looking to test new waters. She always had an obsession for documentaries and loved reading narrative feature pieces but never had the opportunity to actually write one. She has interned at an Indonesian television station, B-Channel TV and the North American International Livestock Exposition. In summer 2013, she also worked at CBS on "Dr. Phil." She will graduate in 2014.

18

For the sake of a dream

By Jordan Sward

One o'clock cannot come fast enough.

It's 8:30 on an autumn Wednesday morning and Heather Smith has a decaf pot in one hand and regular in the other. The five-stool bar at Merry Ann's Diner on Neil Street is occupied by men in Carhartts and camo hats, all of whom Heather addresses by name as she tops off their ceramic coffee mugs.

"Gonna be quiet around here," the cook jokes as he pours liquid eggs on the sizzling skillet. After 1 p.m., there won't be any more dings from Heather's pink cellphone. No more "Hey, Heather" shouts from around the room or the sound of her subtle Indiana twang joking with the regulars.

In her usual uniform of jeans, tennis shoes and a Merry Ann's T-shirt, 25-year-old Heather delivers plates of hash browns and eggs, as she has done for seven years. Today, she delivers them for the last time and she attaches to every handwritten tab a business card: Smith Design & Consign, Heather's new shop at 41 E. University Ave., Suite 1E, which is marked by her fancy new $4,000 black awnings, in downtown Champaign across from the bus station.

Before this morning, she has kept her plans to open the store quiet. After all, she still needs all the income she can get.

"This is the last morning I'll be waiting on you," she tells a booth of four men she has served numerous times. "I'm opening my own store on Thursday."

"Where's this?"

"What kind of a business you got?"

"What's parking like over there?"

"Hope it goes well."

For the few customers who voice their opinions, some fearfully cite the bad economy, some suggest staying open later than her 5 p.m. plan, some tell her she's absolutely nuts. She just smiles and says, "OK."

When the clock strikes 1, Heather counts the tips neatly packed in a plastic cup, which is particularly full today thanks to unusually generous customers, says

Photo by Robin Scholz/The News-Gazette

goodbye to her coworkers and walks out the door to a new and uncertain future.

"You have to take risks if you want to make it anywhere in life," she says.

Heather grew up in and out of foster homes. She remembers moving from home to home — sometimes with her sister, sometimes not — before returning again to her mother's. The day before her 15th birthday, after yet another altercation with her mom, she left to join the already established family of her father, his wife and their daughter. That lasted until just before her last year of high school, when she moved to a house in Rantoul by herself. Every day she woke up, drove to school, then worked until 10 p.m. as a telemarketer.

"That part made me grow up," she says.

Heather planned to attend college to become an interior designer, but she got some unexpected news: She was pregnant. She had a daughter, married and had another daughter. Her dreams of going to college faded, but her passion for interior design never did. All her energy went toward trying to be a better parent than she believed her own parents had been. Yet her free time was spent reading about opening a business and decorating friends' houses and apartments.

She would lie awake thinking about a project, planning in her head exactly where to locate the furniture, what to put on the tables — down to every last lamp and picture frame. If she had to pick any job in the world, she would be an interior designer. Heather's dream was to open her own store. She begged her then-husband to tour vacant retail spaces. He said no; it was too much of a financial risk.

"I felt like I would never be able to be happy. It was almost like I was trapped. I'd be a waitress forever, make decent money, work three days a week — I have time with my kids, but that's not all that I wanted to be."

When she and her husband separated, Heather was "at a really low place." What was she going to do with her life?

"It was all or nothing," she says. "I have to do it now or I know I'm not gonna do it."

She fell in love with the first rental space she saw, filled out an application and rushed it back to the realtor. In August, she took the $15,000 from her divorce settlement and signed a 26-month lease for $1,500 a month.

"Oh, my gosh, what did I do?" she thought.

It's 8:37 the morning of the Big Day — wintry outside, not quite sunny, not quite cloudy. It's like a new Heather who arrives at the store before its 8 a.m. opening. Her shoulder-length blonde hair is straight and little hip, and subtle makeup highlights her hazel eyes. Her diner uniform is gone, replaced with black dress pants, sweater, high heels and a tasteful necklace. Furniture and décor fill the 1,500-square-foot store, most of which Heather bought at estate sales and other shops or online. For four months, she searched for items to refinish, vowing to always sell them in better condition than she bought them in.

A red vase and framed picture sit atop a redone dark cherry entertainment center, matched nicely by the burgundy wall behind it. The store is organized by rooms. A real bamboo chair and couch, accented by seashell candles and a standing light fixture, make up the sun room area. The boy's room features a plain wood dresser, which she painted navy and white with red knobs to match firetruck decor. A hand-painted antique buffet with a red and black design sits next to a framed Marilyn Monroe picture in the retro corner.

Heather has accomplished one of her goals: Smith Design & Consign is not a used junk store. It is the perfectionist image from her dreams. She worries that the paint on the walls turned out a bit streaky. She worries that the spider she discovered last week, the one she's deathly afraid of, is spinning webs somewhere. She worries that the music — from Taylor Swift to Jay-Z — is too loud. She worries that, despite the flashy new awnings, people won't be able to find her place tucked on the second floor behind Kane & Co. Salon and Spa.

Just before her shop opens officially at 9, her first customer arrives: a woman she has served at Merry Ann's. Then two women from the Chamber of Commerce come in to shoot first-day promotional photos, followed by a man with giant ribbon-cutting scissors. Before long, the store is filled with people browsing and chatting. One woman uses her foot to destroy a web the dreaded spider has spun overnight.

"I'll give them 10 more minutes, then we'll take it without them," Heather says of friends who promised to join in the ribbon-cutting ceremony. The chamber crowd congregates for the photo — and one of her friends arrives just in time. Heather holds the theatrical scissors up to the long, shiny red ribbon, giggling in excitement. She's surprised when the oversized scissors actually cut.

At that moment, she has finally made it. She's $200 short on rent that's due on the day of the opening, hoping an expected check will reach her account by the weekend, hoping she will make enough money in the first few days to make it to next week.

She doesn't know how she'll restock the store if everything sells quickly. Or how she will afford the rent on her own apartment. Or food, school costs, utilities or car payments. What if she doesn't meet the $150-a-day profit goal she has set for herself to barely get by?

She doesn't know. But today, she has her eyes on the prize.

If she fails, she'll cut it all for a loss — a loss of all the money she has — and get a job. But no matter what, she's "gonna be one strong frickin' person by the time this is all done."

She dreams of the store's success and telling people: "I just got through a divorce. I just opened a store. I'm raising two kids. I don't need your help."

As the store quiets down, her friend and an old diner customer remain, chatting near the counter. The door swings open, and Heather gasps in giddy surprise. It's Tom Hess, a high school teacher and Heather's new love interest, carrying a box of chocolate-covered strawberries.

"Why aren't you teaching?" she asks.

"I had some really important errands to run," he says with a smile.

Heather is charmed.

It is, she hopes, all her dreams beginning.

Jordan Sward is originally from the small town of Byron, Ill., but now calls the Chicago suburbs her home. She graduated from the University of Illinois with a degree in news-editorial journalism in 2013. She currently works as editorial community manager for Prime Publishing, LLC in Northbrook, Ill. Jordan got her start as a journalist at the Daily Illini, where she was a features reporter. Eventually, she worked her way up to features editor, with various other titles along the way. During her undergraduate career, she also contributed to IMPULSE magazine and HerCampus.com. She also spent a summer in Emmaus, Pa., working as an intern at Men's Health magazine, where she reported and wrote front-of-book pieces and contributed to the book The 8-Hour Diet.

Photo by Robin Scholz/The News-Gazette

19

Not ready for heaven yet

By Samantha Bakall

Willie T. Summerville sits behind the church organ, his fingers dancing on the keys and his lips slightly pursed at the microphone, ready to sing. He does not need his hands to conduct. His elbows, shoulders and upper body serve as the signaling baton. His close-cropped hair is sprinkled salt and pepper, showing his 67 years against his dark skin. His large, grandfather-esque bifocal glasses overshadow the rest of his face, but through the thick lenses, his eyes are smiling.

"Jesus, Jesus, Jesus, what a wonder You are ..." the choir echoes after Mr. Summerville's lead, as the organ rises forth, full and authoritative, modulating up a key. The choir members are old, young, white, black, lifelong Christians and recent born-agains. Some of them sing at the top of their lungs, others are shy and almost mute. For some, this is their first choir rehearsal. Others have grown up in church choirs, just like he did.

"Beautiful rose of Sharon, what a wonder You are ..."

"Somebody say, 'Amen,'" Mr. Summerville dictates to the group in his raspy and resonant voice above the low drone of the receding organ. "We come every week to be unified and offer God something that should be offered for him, in decency and in order." Eruptions of "Praise the Lord" and "Amen" follow.

Thursday evening choir rehearsal at Urbana's Canaan Baptist Church is just one weekly activity that fills Mr. Summerville's busy schedule. His daily alarm goes off at 6 a.m. In fasting season, the day starts with Bible study and prayer. His grandson has band practice at 6:50 a.m. Regular Bible study and group prayer is on Wednesday nights. He also has to prepare for his Monday evening class — "Harmonizing Differences using African American Sacred Music" — at the University of Illinois. Meetings and doctor appointments are ever present, as are funeral services to play for, reference letters to write and rehearsals to conduct.

In his busy schedule, Mr. Summerville doesn't spend much time reflecting on his mortality. In fact, he is pretty confident he's on God's saved list.

Born in Sunshine, Ark., near the Louisiana-Mississippi state line, Mr. Summerville has lived what he calls a "blessed" life. He was the middle child of five born to Moses and Lenora Summerville. The only boy. He grew up in Crossett, a town about 40 miles west of Sunshine. His father was a lumber mill worker, church choir director and a quartet singer. His mother was a cook whose lemon sour cream cake was so good it has been passed down several generations. All the children had to sing and participate in church at least until they moved out of the house.

"Being in the choir was not an option," he says, laughing.

Music and faith in Jesus Christ have been ways of life for him, and sources of comfort, ever since he was a little boy. He learned piano from his father and started playing at church when he was 14. He can quote numerous scriptures off the top of his head, knowledge he refers to as "an insurance policy I'm walking around with that's paid up."

He is also one of Champaign-Urbana's best-known citizens, a literal icon in the sacred music community. After attending the UI for his master's degree in music education, he spent three years teaching music in the Champaign public schools and 35 years in Urbana's schools. This year marks his 34th year at Canaan Baptist and his 45th year at St. Luke's Christian Methodist in Champaign. He has participated in more than 80 workshops and clinics at churches, universities and Air Force bases all over the country and world. He is even asked to occasionally hum a few bars at city council meetings.

"You know what will make you known with people and you don't even be trying to?" he asks. "Serve the people. There's so much to do; it's that kind of involvement. I've been blessed. There have been people who have shown me how much they appreciate my work."

For once, Mr. Summerville is not sitting behind an organ. He stands tall, proud, in his dark brown suit, while rows of white-topped and black-bottomed clad singers file silently past him onto the stage, ready to sing. The audience sits, patiently waiting for the last person to walk on stage. Mr. Summerville is taking it all in. He finally ambles up the aisle of the church, taking time to greet members in the audience and acknowledge his colleagues. By the time he reaches the front, the choir is ready and it is time to sing.

The friendly man who leisurely strolled to the front of the room is transformed. He raises his arms swiftly, in one gesture, and cues the organist to begin. Within the first few measures of the opening song, he is part of the choir. His age disappears. He conducts with such joy and fury that his energy outshines that of many young choir members. He dances to the music, letting every chord progression and modulation guide his movements and lift his spirit. He is a show unto himself.

In this moment, it is just Willie T. Summerville, the music and Jesus.

Mr. Summerville has believed he is going to heaven since he was saved in elementary school. But he's not in any sort of rush — too many things still left for him to do here on earth, and too many people who depend on him.

"I know that I do a lot of things that people depend on me," he says. "And I don't know if others would be as passionate about doing them if I was asked to go to heaven earlier." Christians, he says, do not look at retirement like regular people do. Retirement for them — for him — is heaven. "If I have health and strength, I want to be serving and helping others, and I do that."

Mr. Summerville is thankful for the little things. At his age, many of his contemporaries are in nursing homes and hospitals, but he is still able to get around easily, drive his car and maintain his vision, he says, thanks to God.

"I want to live out my life and do what He tells me He wants me to do," Mr. Summerville says. "I don't treat going to heaven like gambling."

Born and raised in Chicago, Ill., Samantha Bakall became fond of one of the city's most iconic legacies: meat. Naturally, she came to love the rest of the things on the plate as she got older. During her college years, she wrote about food and its place in society. She spent three years with buzz magazine. She started as a food-and-drink writer, moved up to food-and-drink editor, and finished as editor-in-chief. She graduated from the University of Illinois in 2013 with a dual degree in news-editorial journalism and Italian. She now spends her days making craft spirits as an intern at FEW Spirits in Evanston, Ill., and writing about food, travel and food culture for Hogsalt in Chicago. You can find Samantha's musings and food photography at her blog: deepfriedandfrosted.tumblr.com.

Photo by Robin Scholz/The News-Gazette

20

Gone in an instant

By Aubrey Morse

The examination room is bright with fluorescent light, and the tools and stainless steel table shine with a glittery brilliance. Lying on the table is a woman who didn't realize she would die today. The welcome party includes a pathologist, with recorder in hand, and his assistant, who is fastening the strap of a camera around his neck. Pieces of clothing are gently removed. The examination is conducted in a respectful manner. Those in the room know this woman could be a mother, daughter, sister, friend. Although life no longer lights her eyes, she is treated as a person. Champaign County Coroner Duane Northrup stands a few feet away from the table.

"I just never know what's going to happen, and it's always something a little bit different," he says later. "Even deaths that are similar are not 100 percent the same, which keeps it interesting. That's one of the things I like about the job: Every case is a little bit different."

By appearances, the 42-year-old Northrup is an intimidating figure. His muscular build comes complete with broad shoulders. At 6-foot-2, he towers above the pathology staff. Yet, with just the flash of a smile, Northrup instills a sense of warmth and serenity, essential traits in his profession.

Northrup deals with death — "the deceased" — and aspects of life most people would rather avoid. The job is his passion, and he wouldn't trade it for the world. To him, every day is a new adventure, a new case to solve. The job has taught him this: life is precious, and it can be taken away in an instant.

Northrup can't remember every case; he signs off on hundreds each year. But sometimes, when a person walking toward him at the mall or pumping gas two cars down meets his eyes, he knows they have met before because of the death of someone he does not recall.

"I can tell by the look in their face and the response," he says. "The reason being is because they probably didn't know me before the death, but when the death occurred, that's how I came into their life."

For them it was likely one of the worst times in their lives. For Northrup, it was part of the job, a job that's glamorized and simplified into hourlong TV programs such as "CSI: Crime Scene Investigation" and "Body of Proof," among others that have created a public fascination with investigating death.

"I don't know how you do what you do," people often tell him.

Or, "I could never do that."

He smiles, thinking, "My wife's in public education; I could never do what she does, either."

Northrup likes to correct the misconceptions that surround his work. Some of what appears on screen happens in real life, but not much. The science is rarely as complicated as on those TV dramas. Few deaths involve a crime; most are natural. Autopsies? They're conducted by physician pathologists, not coroners, who don't need a medical degree.

Northrup, for instance, has an associate's degree in criminal justice from Parkland College. As coroner, he investigates and rules on the cause and manner of violent or traumatic deaths, sudden or unexpected deaths, unusual deaths, and any death that is unattended by a physician.

Northrup's office sees 1,400 to 1,600 cases a year. He estimates that he regularly clocks 60 hours a week in return for his yearly salary of $86,328. Sometimes, eight or nine cases can come in 24 hours. From 4:30 p.m. to 8:30 a.m., his pager can go off four, five, maybe even six times.

"Hopefully, one or two of those come before you go to bed at whatever time and then you probably have two or three overnight while you're trying to sleep," he says. "It's not so bad if they come close together, but if they come spread out by about two hours or an hour and a half, then you feel like you haven't slept at all."

The list of to-dos after a death is long:

Interview the family.

Order medical records.

Write case narrative.

Get toxicology samples ready.

Yet the most difficult part of any case is the notification: telling the members of a family that their loved one is dead. As Northrup walks to the door, he knows what can happen: Shock. Anger. Disbelief. Tears. Screams. People usually want to know if the person suffered or if the death was instant. He knows what they want to hear, but Northrup will never lie to a family.

"If I can't say with any degree of certainty that I don't believe they suffered, I won't tell them that. I don't want them to get some other opinion or result later that says the opposite. I always hope that something in the autopsy or something that I've determined through the investigation can answer that question and answer it the way they want it to be answered because nobody wants me to say, 'Yes, they suffered.' I can't always tell them that they died instantly."

Back in the autopsy room, the pathologist describes his observations into a small black recorder: "Five feet, two inches (comma) Cold (period) ... Dried Blood (period)."

CLICK. The assistant's camera captures the moment.

The pathologist takes note of everything from the color of the nail polish on the woman's toes to the hydration of her skin. It's a methodical procedure, almost trancelike. Today, he finds no trauma, no exterior injuries and no obvious reason the woman died. An incision is made along her collarbone. Skin is pulled back revealing ribs, organs, and, possibly, the answer. Northrup walks to the other side of the room and flips a switch turning on a vent. He remains in the autopsy suite just in case questions arise or an interesting twist comes about.

"This person may have a congenital heart defect that could be hereditary, and we want to pass that along to the family," he says later. "It may not have anything to do with cause of death; it may be cause of death. Either way, we're going to pass that on to the family later."

It has been almost 11 years since Northrup's first autopsy. After withdrawing from Southern Illinois University at age 19, Northrup returned home to Rantoul to earn a paycheck. He quickly found work in construction and, later, on a farm. He was earning a good living, but he wanted more. Working by day and studying by night, he earned his degree. While thumbing through the classifieds one day in 2001, he happened upon a part-time deputy coroner job for Champaign County. After his second interview, Northrup got the job. That same day, the late Roger Swaney, the coroner at the time, put the new guy through a test.

"Hey, c'mon, we're just about to start an autopsy," Swaney said. "We're going to take you in and see how you do."

Northrup, unsure of what to expect, walked in to see that the pathologist and his assistant had just begun. It all fascinated Northrup. The autopsy procedures, the quest for understanding, the puzzle of it all. Northrup didn't become ill. He didn't become faint. That impressed Swaney.

Two years later, Swaney asked Northrup, then a full-time deputy coroner, to run for the elected office from which he was retiring. Northrup began appearing in parades, at pancake breakfasts and on people's doorsteps. He won election in 2004 and '08. He will be on the ballot again in November. The job has changed him, made him far more appreciative of every minute a person has in this world.

"It can all change in an instant," now runs through his mind constantly and makes him worry far more about matters he can't control. For instance, his oldest daughter is in her teens and will be driving soon, a troubling fact for a man who sees innumerable auto fatalities. Already, she's going out with friends who drive. When his phone rings with word of a teen crash fatality, everything halts.

"My heart stops for a few seconds, and I have to pause and think, and I just tell myself, 'I hope it's not them.' " He knows that in most cases he's working, the victims got up in the morning, said "Goodbye" to their spouses and children, gave each a kiss and went off to work or school or shopping. It's unsettling to realize that he is going to show up and report that the person is now dead.

"And they didn't have a clue that was going to happen," he says. "Of course, nobody did."

The knowledge makes him truly value a laugh shared between him and his staff, a pleasantly unexpected phone call from his wife, the 30 minutes he got to see his three daughters this morning.

"I'm trying to make more of an effort to have more moments like that," he says solemnly.

Today's autopsy has concluded. The pathologist removes his gloves and Northrup gathers medical samples for transport to the lab. Of the job, he says, "It's taught me to cherish the time I do have with my family more because of what I see."

As he constantly reminds himself, "It can all change in an instant."

Aubrey Morse, a graduate of the University of Illinois with a bachelor's degree in broadcast journalism, is from Urbana, Ill. Her experiences in journalism are rich and diverse. She has worked in an array of media, from print to television. Aubrey currently serves as the on-air midday personality on WDNL-FM and WSOY-FM. She also works as a news videographer for WCIA-TV.

21

Music is his life

By Samantha Kiesel

Chip McNeill walks down the hall in his black sneakers as jazz music floods the basement of Smith Hall. He waves with his left hand to a couple of students and clutches a soprano saxophone in his right. He looks at his watch and picks up his pace, realizing he's late. In Room 11, a small space with a set of drums, a piano and an old organ, he gently places his instrument on the organ bench as he greets the students preparing for the day's jazz rehearsal.

The drummer tunes his instruments, the guitarist adjusts the volume on his amplifier, the vocalist tinkers with her mic, the saxophonist fixes his reed, and the piano player sits patiently. Chip, a 51-year-old University of Illinois jazz professor in his 11th year, adjusts his Levis and rolls up the sleeves of his black turtleneck. He is about to start class when the saxophonist receives a text from a missing student, the bass player. He woke up late and will be here ASAP.

"I mean, come on," Chip says with a laugh. "If I can get here, you can get here."

His mother was a vocalist, and his father was a saxophonist. Music is the first thing Chip remembers, specifically jazz records playing in his house. He was exposed to all kinds of music, but jazz was his favorite. As with many career musicians, it all started with the piano, and Chip began playing at age 6.

At 15, he started playing the saxophone. When he played the sax it was like an extension of his voice, an organic sound. Air goes in and music comes out, creating something out of nothing. He was hooked.

"They are like my toys, my favorite toys," Chip says of his saxophones. "I'll never outgrow them. They've always been that, and they always will be."

Chip couldn't imagine becoming anything other than a professional jazz performer. It was the only career path he considered. Nothing fascinated him as much as jazz music. He needed to play. He certainly never thought of teaching.

"Performing is a part of me," he says.

Photo by Robin Scholz/The News-Gazette

SLICES OF LIFE

The students discuss the music they're writing, as Chip sits quietly on the organ bench. They are about to start playing a song written by the saxophonist. He just finished it last night, so the flow is rough.

"Let's take it slower than necessary until we get a handle of the notes," Chip says in a friendly tone. He then takes a look at the sheet music and challenges the saxophonist.

"In the second bar, you have an A-flat in the bass and an A-sus chord."

"Yeah, it's messed up," the sax player says.

"Well, don't say that. What do you want? You want an A-flat in the bass?"

"No, I want an A in the bass."

"OK, that looks fine. Let's play."

At that moment, the bass player walks in.

"Better late than never," Chip says.

Chip is no stranger to rehearsals. He toured with jazz legends Woody Herman, Maynard Ferguson and Arturo Sandoval. He started touring with Herman the day he earned his master's from Miami University. Despite being married, Chip took the gig that would force him on the road for six months at a time.

"When gigs come along like that, you take them," he says.

Chip doesn't remember specific performances. With so many in the last 30 years, they are a blur. But he remembers the places he traveled: Japan, Europe, India, Australia. He remembers Carnegie Hall, Royal Albert Hall, the Sydney Opera House. He remembers the music he wrote, particularly when he was musical director for Ferguson and wrote music that always left room for instrumental solos. Solos allow musicians to be "in the moment," so immersed in the music that they forget all about technique, practice and experience. It's what Chip calls "pure expression." At those moments, his saxophone is an extension of his body.

"The moment I step on the stage, I stay in the moment and in the present," he says. "Otherwise I can't give all of myself to my music."

Once the tardy bass player is ready, the combo picks up again. The music is starting to work. The solos are fluid, the bridge is connected to the chorus and the students are enjoying themselves.

"You're plenty active during the melody," Chip tells the drummer. "In fact, I think you can play that a little quieter. Make more out of each of the phrases."

The guitarist chimes in with some new chords.

"Yeah, there you go," Chip says. "That's the right idea. We're getting there."

When Chip hears great musicians — say, John Coltrane — he hears time spent. Time spent creating a tone or a sound, time spent rehearsing, time spent perfecting a personal style.

That's the challenge: discovering your own style. It's impossible for musicians to immediately decide on their style. It takes experience, practice and countless mistakes. Chip doesn't try to emulate his heroes, but he takes pieces from the likes of Coltrane and translates them into his own. Developing your sound is like creating your own voice.

The musician uses the notes like a painter uses a palette of colors, mixing and matching notes. The musician uses the work of other players and his own personal experiences in creating a sound no one has heard.

"The sound is in the ear of the beholder," Chip says.

It takes sacrifice to find that special sound. Chip spent decades searching for his sound. He spent holidays and birthdays away from his wife and family. In the end, the marriage failed. He has no children. All of his close friends are musicians. Music is his life.

"I probably would have had a family if I did something else, if I was a plumber or something," he says. "People go home and leave their work at work. Here, with this, you don't, ever. Music is like any art. You never leave it; you're constantly practicing to get better at it. Because you have to."

Chip never planned to be a teacher. In fact, he was anti-teaching. Music wasn't learned in a classroom, he believed. It was learned through those hours and years of experience.

"I did most of my learning myself, I have to say. Even though I had good teachers along the way, I probably didn't take advantage of them enough," he says. "I took advantage of the fact that jazz allowed me to learn myself."

Yet it was time for a break, despite his love for performing, and he took a teaching job at Virginia Tech University, where his then-wife was a vocal professor. The stable income drew him in. Eventually, he accepted his teaching position at the University of Illinois, where as head of the jazz studies program in the School of Music he would create the bachelor's, master's and doctoral programs in jazz performance. Although teaching has its financial advantages and allows Chip to be selective when choosing gigs, it also came with a surprising dividend:

"The biggest thing I've enjoyed is seeing the success of students."

The room is jamming by the end of class. The music the saxophonist wrote finally has a groove to it, and Chip has come alive. His feet tap to the tempo, his head bobs and even swoops when a great phrase is played. With 10 minutes left in class, Chip places his hand on his soprano saxophone. He is wondering if he should pick it up. He takes off the reed cap, then replaces it. But with two minutes left, he can't resist. The funky groove pairs the guitar and saxophone in sync, and the deep lower chords of the bass draw him in.

"Play the vamp a couple times," he says. "I just want to play with you guys for a minute."

And Chip dives into a solo. After a long high note, a series of uncountable notes follows and progresses into a half-a-minute solo. His face turns from pale to red. His eyes stay closed and his head faces the floor. Then he abruptly waves the combo to stop. He tells everybody they need to play with more confidence. He suggests some different chords to the guitar player. He tells the bass player to be clearer about the notes he's playing.

"Ya dig?" Chip asks.

They dig.

Samantha Kiesel is from St. Charles, Ill. She graduated from the University of Illinois in 2013 with a bachelor's in news-editorial journalism. When she was a freshman, she joined The Daily Illini. During her four years there, she worked as an assistant sports editor and as the men's basketball beat writer. She was the editor-in-chief of the paper her senior year. She has interned at the Daily Herald in Arlington Heights, Ill. After graduating, she worked as a sports copy editing intern at the Chicago Tribune. She currently works for Shaw Media as a copy editor and page designer.

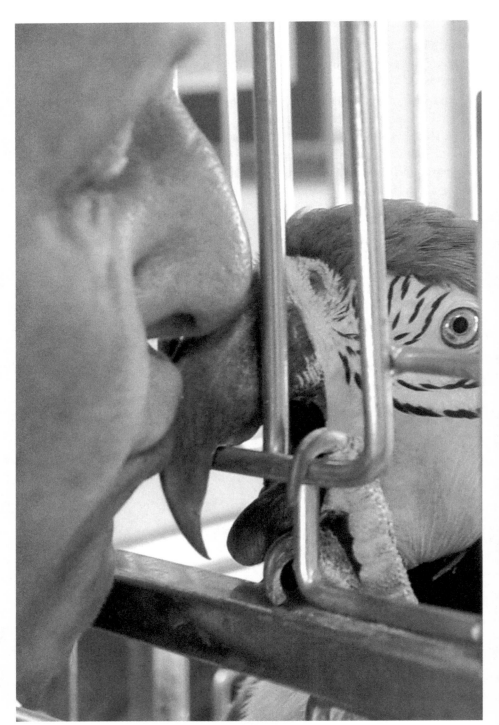

Photo by Robin Scholz/The News-Gazette

SLICES OF LIFE
116

22

For the love of birds

By Jessica Bourque

Cindy Eaglen — that's eagle with an "n" — sits in her computer chair, a bird in one hand, a mouse in the other. The mouse is of the computer variety, but the bird is an African grey, one of the smartest avian breeds in the animal kingdom. Cindy carefully holds the two, kissing one on the beak and using the other to scroll through YouTube videos; she is searching for one of her favorites.

"It's amazing!" she says. "They put on some NSYNC song or something (It's actually Backstreet Boys.) and this bird starts dancing — just bobbing his head and moving his feet perfectly in line with the beat!"

She finds the video, and soon a cockatoo named Snowball appears on the screen.

"Look at him! Isn't he …?" she seems about to finish that thought with "amazing" or "incredible," but she's interrupted.

"Ow!"

That's Pretty — the bird perched so contentedly on Cindy's hand who wants back in the spotlight. He likes being the center of attention and doesn't want to compete with this virtual counterpart now dancing, quite rhythmically, to the boy-band hit "Backstreet's Back."

"Ow?! Well, nobody hurt you! What are you 'Ow-ing' about?" Cindy replies.

She speaks to her birds in high-pitched coos, much like a mother humoring a jabbering toddler. It's appropriate, really. Cindy considers her birds to be an extension of her family. She knows they can't replace her two daughters or her husband, but all 13 of her "feathered children" who live at her house provide a companionship Cindy hasn't found in any other animal. These birds are her passion. Her obsession started with a heart attack. Cindy smoked most her life, and 12 years ago, at age 50, she finally paid for it. The heart attack meant Cindy had to stop smoking for good, but she couldn't rely on her weak willpower. She had to find help.

"I want a bird," she told her husband.

Birds are unique creatures in that they have air sacs instead of lungs, which means they can die upon inhaling tobacco smoke. Cindy realized that with birds she shared a common enemy: cigarettes. This vulnerability made a bird "the perfect insurance plan" in Cindy's struggle to stop smoking. That Mother's Day, she bought a blue and gold macaw named Anton.

"They can express their affection verbally. I have birds that tell me, 'I love you. I love your kisses,' and I know they mean it."

She pauses to shower Pretty in tender pecks on the beak.

"Yes, your momma loves you, doesn't she?"

Affection, humor, profanity: her birds articulate it all. In fact, they hardly shut up. It's not uncommon to hear Bo, Cindy's gold and blue cockatoo, scream a familiar obscenity when she is frustrated — a bad habit she picked up from Cindy. Or Susanna, a scarlet red macaw, shout, "Goonie birds!" when she feels silly. The term, borrowed from Susanna's favorite show, Sesame Street, is an inside joke among Susanna and her dozen cage mates. Anytime she says it, the birds will erupt in laughter, which, to the untrained ear, is really just squawking and screeching.

That laughter reverberates throughout the spacious, well-lit room that houses Susanna, Bo, Bella, Howard, Murphy, Heidi, Muffin, Scarlet, Gracie, Benny (short for Benjamin Franklin), Captain Morgan, Bandit and Cleo. In this room — a special addition to Cindy's Danville home that she built specifically for her birds — they spend their days perching in expensive cages, watching their favorite cartoons and getting pampered. For Cindy's babies, no amenities are skimped.

Terry, Cindy's recently retired husband, does a lot of the caretaking. Cindy works a day job managing the couple's two waste management businesses, Gotta Potty and Illini Recycling. But even at her office, located on the outskirts of Champaign, Cindy is surrounded by exotic birds. The small space doubles as the headquarters for her avian rescue operation, Feathered Friends. The 6-year-old organization is run by Cindy and Terry. Their goal is simple: Rescue abandoned or mistreated birds and find them loving, permanent homes.

Because exotic birds have a lifespan of about 70 years, it's difficult to find eternal housing for the castaways. People often tire of the loud pets after a few years. So Cindy doesn't allow just any Joe Blow to adopt her birds — they must be perfect fits.

"Well, you don't even care if I take a bird, do you?!" accused one potential parent, irritated with Cindy's background check.

"No, I don't," Cindy retorted. "I do this entirely for the birds, not for the people."

Cindy estimates that she "re-homes" about 70 birds a year. As of now, 20 orphans — including Pretty — populate her rescue. She travels all over the Midwest to rescue her birds, but there is no distance she wouldn't travel; she has flown as far as California for a bird, and she'd do it again.

Sometimes, the birds come to her. After one African grey boarded at Cindy's rescue, the bird's parent complained: "Murphy hasn't been the same since we picked him up. All day he just sits in the washing machine and only comes out once a day to bite me." It was decided that Murphy was simply happier with Cindy, so he became a member of her flock. Now, the cantankerous bird that sat in the washing machine all day is one of the friendliest of Cindy's birds.

"Are you going to pop for momma?" Cindy asks, playing Murphy's favorite game.

To the uninitiated, it seems she is just talking nonsense with Murphy; but really, she's playing an elaborate game, one she thinks proves Murphy's supreme intelligence. If Murphy is happy, he dips his body, bobs his head and makes an impeccable "pop" noise, which he does now.

"Oo! Thank you! Are you happy to see momma today?"

Today's game is half fun, half preparation. Cindy is readying Murphy for a public showing. She seizes every chance to show off of her charismatic creatures to rectify "the serious misunderstandings" people have about birds.

Today, the presentation is at the Champaign County Humane Society and the audience is a group of children. Murphy should be a hit; kids love the antics of Cindy's birds. But the room turns out to be small, and Murphy is gnawing at his claws, a sign he is nervous. Cindy never forgets the possibility of disaster, even if it is unlikely. If Murphy bites, claws or, God forbid, poops on a child, the presentation, along with everyone's perception of birds, could be irreparably marred.

Cindy has heard all the accusations: Birds are loud, stupid, annoying, a hassle. But when she witnesses her birds singing opera, creating nicknames, telling jokes, expressing affection, even giving kisses — she knows the bird haters are wrong.

"They are truly the most misunderstood creatures. .. They say birds have an intelligence comparable to that of apes and dolphins! But they have discipline of a 2-year-old."

Murphy is still biting at his talons as he and Cindy wait for the children to arrive. Cindy is sitting on a stool toward the front of the room when her phone goes off; she grips onto Murphy. Even unexpected noises like a phone-ring can spook him. She checks it.

"Oh! It's just Murphy," she chuckles. "He has learned to imitate the beep on my Nextel!"

He can also do a back-up beeper on a garbage truck and a drop of water "so convincing it makes me get up and check the faucet."

The kids pour in making a sea of bright red shirts.

"Wheeee woooo," Murphy whistles playfully.

The children explode with high-pitched laughter. But it isn't until halfway through the presentation that Murphy really starts his display. He loosens his feet from Cindy's grip and takes a few laps around the room. This time, the laughter is a thin veil hiding the children's fear.

"He's just putting on a show for you all!" Cindy reassures them.

Cindy wraps up the presentation quickly. Two birds are on their way to her rescue. She knows them well because she raised them before they were adopted by new parents. Now, their owner is ill and can't care for them anymore. Cindy's budget is tight, but she will still take them.

"I will make it work. I always do."

As she leaves, she inundates Murphy with praise and affection. He ruffles his feathers, a sign that he's happy, says Cindy — no one understands Murphy's mannerisms quite like she does.

"It takes so very little to make them happy and, in turn, their biggest desire in this world is to make you happy. Like Murphy here. I know Murphy loves me so much. I know there is nothing he wouldn't do for me."

And that is enough for Cindy.

Jessica Bourque graduated from the University of Illinois in 2013 with a degree in news-editorial journalism. Her work has been published by the New York Times, The News-Gazette, buzz magazine, CU-CitizenAccess.org, the Midwest Center for Investigative Reporting and Latitude News. She has written about almost everything — from cockatoos to clowns to carbon emissions. Her primary interests are in social and environmental justice. When she isn't reporting, Jessica is a freelance writer for The Nature Conservancy. Jessica's career has taken her from her small, hog-farming hometown of Kewanee, Ill., to faraway places such as Istanbul.

Acknowledgements

Champaign-Urbana is fortunate to have a newspaper whose employees and management care deeply about its content, mission and community. For that, I thank *The News-Gazette* board members, publisher and staffers. For this project specifically, thanks goes to publisher John Foreman, who helped conceive of the collaborative classroom and then encouraged his editorial staff to take part. Thanks to the paper's features editor Tony Mancuso, who shepherded each story for the "Slice of Life" series through to publication as covers of the paper's Sunday Living section. Thanks to *News-Gazette* photographers Darrell Hoemann, Heather Coit, John Dixon, Robin Scholz and Bradley Leeb, whose photos made our story subjects come to life. Thanks to Joan Millis, *News-Gazette* graphic artist, who designed the book. Thanks to University of Illinois Department of Journalism Head Rich Martin and College of Media Dean Jan Slater for encouraging the collaboration from the beginning. Thanks to Department of Journalism graduate student research assistant Robert Holly for tracking down my former and present students and collecting and editing their bios.

Special thanks to the Marajen Stevick Foundation for supporting the project.

Finally, thanks to the University of Illinois journalism students who diligently reported, wrote and rewrote their stories to meet a high professional standard. I treated them as if they were young reporters working for me at *The Washington Post,* which means with considerable tough love. Yet their talent and commitment to excellence is all their own. We will hear from these young men and women in the future — and be glad we knew them on the way up.

W.H.

Walt Harrington was a long-time staff writer for *The Washington Post Magazine,* where he wrote numerous benchmark profiles of public notables such as George H.W. Bush, Jesse Jackson, Jerry Falwell and Carl Bernstein, as well as scores of in-depth pieces on ordinary people, including a mentally retarded man, a fundamentalist Christian family and a happily married couple.

His work has won numerous journalism awards, including the Sigma Delta Chi Distinguished Service Award and the Lowell Mellett Award for improving journalism through critical evaluation. His book, *The Everlasting Stream: A True Story of Rabbits, Guns, Friendship, and Family,* became an Emmy-winning PBS documentary film. His book, *Crossings: A White Man's Journey into Black America,* won the Gustavus Myers Award for the Study of Human Rights in the U.S. and was declared a "vital" book on race in America by *The New York Times.* Mr. Harrington is the author or editor of five other nonfiction books, including *American Profiles, At the Heart of It, The Beholder's Eye, Next Wave* and *Intimate Journalism,* which has been widely used in journalism classes around the country.

He is a journalism professor at the University of Illinois at Urbana-Champaign, where he teaches literary feature writing and has served in administrative capacities as journalism department head, associate chancellor and interim dean of the College of Media. He holds masters degrees in sociology and journalism from the University of Missouri-Columbia. More published articles by his students can be found at intimatejournalism.com.